GOD'S
BEST
FRIEND

GABRIEL LOPEZ

THE ADVENTURES OF AN ORDINARY MAN
AND AN EXTRAORDINARY GOD.

If you have ever read even one post on social media from Gabriel Lopez, then I am sure you became an instant follower. His humor, depth and heart are always on full display in his writing. Every time I see that he has written something, I pause and make the time to read it through carefully, his material is truly unique. Like many of you, I have been waiting in eager anticipation for his first book to finally be released and look forward to laughing and crying my way through it. Nothing more needs to be said, simply get your copy of this book and get a few more to give away!

Dr. Jonathan Welton
President of Welton Academy

God's Best Friend is a must read!!! If you want to know the God who "isn't just real" but who is "waiting to take you on the craziest adventures you've ever seen," Gabriel's book will do just that. His vulnerability in sharing how God has journeyed with him in every adventure will stir you to greater depths of intimacy with Jesus. One of the things I love the most is that everything in this book and in Gabriel's life always comes back to a love relationship with God. I highly recommend this book and pray that it marks you with the love and faithfulness of Jesus like never before.

Jennifer A. Miskov, PhD,
Author and founding director of Destiny House

Gabriel's stories of his friendship with God will at times make you laugh and at others make you cry. I have walked with Gabriel and can attest to both his character and gifting. Gabriel Lopez is truly a friend of God. I would venture to say, one of God's best friends. I highly recommend this book as one that will create a greater hunger to hear God's voice and walk with Him every day.

Ivan Roman
www.ivanroman.org

I love Gabriel. He isn't just a great friend and lover of Jesus, he is a wonderful storyteller. In *God's Best Friend* you will read miraculous stories of God's gentle invasion into the daily details of our lives. There is very little that is more encouraging than tangible examples of how this beautiful, invisible God is here with us at every step, every decision, every birth, and every moment. As you read this book you will discover God through a lens of childlike faith that Gabriel has cultivated throughout the years of prayer, relationship, loss, and worship. The page's bleed with the joy and trust of a man that has decided that to embrace this life with the humility and faith of a child. You will be just as quick to laugh as you will to set the book down to give yourself time to reflect upon what you just read, as sometimes the greatest depth is found in the simplicity of the astonishing fact that God is here, with us, and will never stop being a part of our daily lives.

Tyler Johnson
Author, DRT Director
OneGlance.org

When you are leaning into God, the natural fast becomes supernatural. That's what sets Gabriel Lopez apart from many others: His ability to see God's supernatural in what many would pass as coincidence. His stories illustrate and teach us how to engage when God speaks, spurring us onto greater expectation for God to do the impossible in us and through us. I have not only found myself laughing out loud with wonder as I read his encounters, but also, stirred to a deeper confidence in how God leads us into our destiny! This collective of God moments will not only bless and inspire you, it will take you on your own journey of walking into the normal Christian life of signs and wonders. Gabriel is a friend of God and that's what I love about him! In this book, he has invited us into his story with God. You do not want to miss this!

Julian Adams
www.frequentsee.org

God is looking for friends. And Gabriel is one...

Daniel Chalmers and I have had the highest joy and honor of knowing Gabriel and Louise Lopez for the past eight years. They are not only God's beloved friends — but some of ours. Our lives are so much richer thru this covenant friendship. The first time I met Gabriel, an angel came as we prophesied, and a tangible wind of the Holy Spirit marked this sovereign meeting.

Just like this moment, heaven backs their lives, as they walk with God as His friend. When Gabriel and I shot our first romantic comedy together, I had a series of prophetic dreams about how much Jesus treasured Gabriel's voice and to protect him finding that voice as a story teller. When I got hired to direct another documentary, I told the producer only if he hired Gabriel, as Gabriel's voice and ability to hear God's voice has become an irreplaceable part of our lives. He is a story teller, a writer, a prophet and a true friend.

Written in an episodic or devotional adventures with God, this book is an invitation for your own encounter. Each chapter is a like a portal containing more than information but impartation.

Gabriel is a prophet who is also a pastor. He is a prophet of love. And Gabriel is an emerging voice in our generation. He has a profound and powerful personal testimony in this book and a rich deep history in the Lord. This book carries keys that took him decades to earn. May you go on a journey of encountering the heart of the Father who wants to encounter you even more than you do — as you read the pages that lie before you...Gabriel has labored a lifetime for the chapters that await you! As you read, may you put a full demand on heaven to receive everything Jesus died for put a full demand on heaven to receive everything Jesus died for! May this book take you into the height and depth and width and breath of the love of a Good, Good Father who longs to call you His friend.

Shara and Daniel Chalmers
Love Wins Ministries

Bigger on the inside than the outside. That should be the goal for every Seer, mystic, and disciple of Jesus. Gabriel is exactly that. He carries a quiet, infectious, depth of relationship with God that will make you want to hang around him more and listen to his stories more. You will enjoy his clear, authentic stories as he brings you with him on his journey where God pursues him.

Ian Carroll
Ian Carroll Ministries

I have never met anyone who lives and experiences the adventure-filled life of a son of God like Gabriel. His life is a walking testament to the Father's desire to encounter us daily so that we fill the pages of our books with the constant pursuit of His inescapable love. I have been forever marked by sharing in some of these incredible moments where I witnessed the simple yet profound revelation of childlike wonder mixed with faith which has now resulted in the book you have in your hands. It will stir you deeply to leave the shores of mediocrity in your relationship with God and dare you to jump out into the adventure you were created for. The invitation lies in the pages you are about to read.

Nate Johnston
Everyday Revivalists

Gabriel Lopez is a unique and Substantial individual who walks what he talks and practices what he preaches. In hearing from Gabe over the past few years in friendship and partnership in ministry he has always struck me as the type of man I would call the real deal. It isn't often you are given access into someone's intimate and powerful journey as a disciple and in this book, I believe you will meet a man who I have always felt carries with him the ability to create access to the heart of God through his story.

Please read with care as you are being introduced and taken on a journey of sincerity and substance by an emerging voice in the modern-day movement of the kingdom. I highly recommend this book and pray it truly blesses your journey.

Tommy Green
Revolution Reality Ministries

Unless otherwise identified, Scripture quotations marked NIV are taken from the HOLY BIBLE, NEW INTERNATIONAL VERSION, Copyright © 1973, 1978, 1984, 2011 International Bible Society. Used by permission of Zondervan. All rights reserved.

Scripture quotations marked ESV are taken from the ESV ® Bible (The Holy Bible, English Standard Version ®), copyright 2001 by Crossway, a publishing ministry of Good News Publishers. Used by permission. All rights reserved.

All emphasis within Scripture quotations is the author's own.

Cover Art: Gabriel Lopez
Interior Design: Renee Evans

ISBN: 978-1-7321077-0-0

Printed in the United States

ACKNOWLEDGMENTS

My family. Eric Shortle. Tyler Johnson. The Gowan family. Jonathan Welton. Shara & Danny Chalmers. Ivan Roman. Carlos Huertas.

I'm grouping you all together because I gotta keep the word count down to save on costs. Totally kidding. I grouped you together because when I started to thank you individually, the acknowledgment section was turning into the longest chapter of the book. You're all family to me. Every single one of you. I can't thank you enough for believing in me. Each of you has inspired me in ways I can't even begin to describe. You've shaped who I am in God. You've been there on my good days as well as my bad ones. Thank you for always loving me just the way I am. It means more than you will ever know.

And last, but certainly not least, my beautiful wife. This book was born through blood, sweat, tears, and probably 5,000 or more bowls of cereal that you would bring me just because you were thinking of me. How did I get so lucky to marry someone so wonderful as you? You would think that after all that time it would get easier to describe your *love* for someone, but to be honest, as time goes on, it only becomes that much more difficult. It's like the more your love grows, the lesser your ability to explain that love becomes. I think that's why marriage is such a perfect symbolism of who God is. You may think that a million years from now you will finally understand the fullness of God's love. But something tells me we'll just be a million steps further down an endless path. You carry the love of Jesus every single day; just by being you. *I wanna be like you when I grow up.* And that's why anytime I use the word honor in this book, I write it as *honour.* To honour my British bride. Thank you, Sweetie. Love you always.

CONTENTS

FIGHT TO WRITE

Friends and family have encouraged me for years to write a book, but it seemed that no matter how hard I tried I just could never bring myself to do it. As time went on, it was evident that no matter how many people encouraged me, procrastination would always win in the end. One day, I got so fed up with myself that I cried out to God, "What is wrong with me? Help me!" When I said those words, it was like I could feel something buried under all of that procrastination. I sat there for a moment in that feeling; then I asked myself one simple question. 'What am I afraid of?' Instantly, I could feel doubt and fear of failure when thinking about my book. It was then that I knew my procrastination was just a mask for all the fears that were hiding under the surface.

It was encouraging to pinpoint what fears were holding me back, but I still needed the right motivation to move past them. Wanting to write an all-time best seller or making tons of money have never really been big motivators for me to write. And whatever my motivation was, it needed to be bigger than the fears that crippled me. But it seemed like every motivation I came up with wasn't enough to get me past that fear and doubt. I laid on my bed one night wracking my brain trying to think of the right motivation when I finally just gave up. I closed my eyes and drifted off to sleep in a fit of hopelessness. Little did I know the very next morning my motivation would finally arrive.

My eyes shot open, and I quickly sat up in bed. It was quiet, and my alarm hadn't gone off yet, but it was like something had woken me up. I couldn't place my finger on it, but something inside me just felt, different. I sat there scanning the room as if someone had just been there. I eventually laid back down to try and go back to sleep, but I couldn't shake this new feeling. As I laid there, the thought of my book crept back into my head. But this time, instead of fear and doubt, a new thought followed it; my children.

I replayed the thought again in my head. "My children." It was a strange thought to have because we didn't have any children of our own yet. But the more I thought about it, the more I started to realize that if I were to write this book, I would be able to give my children something that I could never give them otherwise; a physical inheritance that carries my voice, my humor, and my heart. But not just my children, I saw it extending even further down the family line. My fingerprints could extend to the generation of my children, my grand-children, my great-grandchildren, and beyond. My life could help steer the course of a lineage that I may never get to see. I started looking at my book like I never had before. I didn't just 'want' to write a book anymore, I absolutely needed to!

This book is dedicated to all of my kids. My children, my grand-children, my great-grandchildren, my spiritual children, and beyond. My prayer is that as you read these pages, you will receive a tangible blessing from God. I pray that you can learn in months what took me years to learn. Every gift, every encounter, every single moment that you read about in this book is available to you. There isn't one story in this book that isn't completely true. I promise you. God is more in-credible and beautiful than we could ever possibly imagine. Remember, YOU were the highest motivation that God gave me. And the days where fear and doubt tried to fight their way back in, I had to hold that motivation close. It wasn't easy; there were hard days and even hard weeks. I had to fight to write! I almost gave up so many times. But that motivation of truth was more powerful than the lie. You, my child, are worth it. Fear and doubt will never rob our family of our inheritance.

You were created to do things that this world has never seen. I believe in you. I have faith in you. Never forget that.

Standing with you always,
Gabriel Lopez

FLOODGATES

My entire life revolved around the church as a child. I went to Sunday school, church camp, and church picnics galore. And since my parents were on the worship team, we were usually the first ones to arrive and the last ones to leave. By the time I turned eighteen, I had spent somewhere around 10,000 hours at church. In my eyes, my whole life embodied from head to toe what it meant to be a Christian. But just because you know every Bible story and have listened to countless Sunday sermons doesn't actually mean that you *know* God at all. And the life I was living on the outside was very different than the life I lived on the inside.

Even though I had grown up in a Christian household my entire life, I was, unfortunately, living two drastically separate lives: my church life and my real life. I was a pro at making sure that these two worlds never collided with each other. It was my *'life of sin'* vs. my *'life of appearance'*. In my teenage years, I became exceptionally good at hiding my secret life. On the outside, you would never have known I was struggling with anything, but just under the surface, I was addicted to pornography and was sexually active. For many years, the back and forth between these two different worlds was fluid and easy. I became exceptionally good at playing church. But one Sunday morning, I experienced something for the first time that I had never seen before in my *normal* Christian life: the hand of God.

It was a regular Sunday morning just like any other. Worship had ended and the pastor got up to speak. My friend and I were in the middle of playing a game where we would find a random word in the room and see how many words we could make from it. So if we saw the word *Yamaha*, on an instrument or something, we would say, "Ham, yam, hay, may, etc." Once we exhausted the word of all possibilities, we would simply move onto whatever next word we could find. We got creative in passing the time. But right as it was my turn to find a new word in the room, the pastor shouted my name out of nowhere. I snapped forward in my seat from the shock. I thought we had been caught, but to my surprise, he began to share to the church what he felt God was going to do in my life. He began to prophesy about how I will go into the film industry and how God is going to give me a mind that creates so much. I was instantly drawn in by the moment; I sat there and listened intently to his words. Just recently, I had begun to develop an interest in the arts that I hadn't shared with anyone. I had no idea how he knew all that about me. As I listened to him prophesy, I thought to myself for the first time, "I think there's more to *God* than I originally thought."

Even though I was living two separate lives at the time, deep down I still believed in God. It was just that my prayer life was very similar to my church life in that it was carved out in routine. My whole relationship with Jesus consisted of three very simple things: apologizing for looking at pornography, promising never to do it again, and then feeling bad for immediately breaking that promise. And since I wasn't the biggest fan of the constant shame that I felt after prayer, I tried to avoid those talks with God as best as I could. But the day I heard the pastor prophesy those things about me in church, something started to shift within me. And my *'secret life'*, that I had kept so well hidden, began to finally unravel at the seems.

I always knew that I was living in sin, it just never bothered me in the slightest. But after that prophetic word, I began waking up with something that I had never felt before: Conviction. And every time that I sinned after that, I didn't just feel *obligated to apologize*, I felt convicted! I tried to ignore it at first, but the more I did, the more that conviction seemed to grow. I didn't know what to do with this new feeling because my whole relationship with God was based on making promises and then immediately breaking them. I had gotten good at living with the shame that I accumulated, but no matter what I did, it was impossible to ignore this conviction.

I started thinking more about the secret life that I had been living. Day and night it sat in my brain; staring at me like it was waiting for me to do something. My conversations with God began to change but not always for the better. I would find myself shouting, "I don't know what you want me to do, God! What are you expecting me to do!?" With every passing day my frustrations grew to new heights, and with that, a different prayer was formed on my lips, "If you want me to change, then show me how." And for the first time in my life, I knew that I had to make a change. I was just utterly clueless on how to do it.

Little did I know that during this season of my life, my sister, Daniella, was praying for me every single day. Even though she didn't know what I was going through, God kept constantly putting me on her heart. She would often ask me how I was doing and my response was always the same, "I'm fine." But deep down I longed to share about my struggles. Then one day, I overheard my parents talking about an event, called *The Call*, that was taking place at Titan Stadium in Nashville, Tennessee. They said there was going to be over 70,000 people at this event worshiping Jesus. For some reason, the moment they mentioned it, my ears instantly perked up. And the more I listened to them talk about it, the more I felt something begin to stir inside my heart. I had no idea why but I had to know more about this strange gathering. I had never been interested in anything like this ever before, or even cared for that matter. My sister became noticeably curious as to why I constantly inquired about the details concerning this event. Then one day out of nowhere she asked me, "Could you ever see yourself going to an event like that?" I replied back, "Uh, I mean, it would be interesting to see it, but I could never imagine myself going to that. I mean, I've never even been on a plane before." She then looked me right in the eyes and said, "If you want to go, I'll go with you." I remember looking back at my sister so shocked. I think Daniella knew deep down that I wanted to go but I wasn't going to volunteer that information freely. And if there's one you should know about me it's this: I love an adventure. And with a big smile, I replied back, "Alright, let's do it."

I couldn't believe I was actually going to Nashville, Tennessee. And to be honest, I still had no idea why I even wanted to do it! I had never been on a *trip* at all before. But something was pulling me towards *The Call*, and I had to see what it was. When I was a child, if I saw a random button, I had to press it to see what happened. If I saw an alley, I had to go down it to investigate. I've always been an inquisitive person by nature. It's definitely gotten me into trouble at times. Even to this day, as an adult, I have to restrain myself from looking behind closed doors when being given a tour of people's homes. The only way I can describe it is that I was experiencing a level of curiosity that I had never felt before. And before I knew it, for the first time in my entire life, I was flying on a plane towards Nashville, Tennessee.

I'll never forget the day of The Call. I walked into Titan Stadium, and was instantly blown away but what I saw. There were already tens of thousands of people worshipping Jesus together. I had never seen anything like it. So-many-people. And even though it was early in the morning when we got there, it was already hot. But not just hot, it was *humid* hot. And it only got hotter, and hotter, and hotter. I've grown up in sunny California my whole life, and I had never experienced heat like this. It was like being stuck in an oven! People were literally passing out in the stadium while they worshipped. Most people were in stands trying to find some sort of shade, but there was also a standing section on the field in the hot sun. I wasn't just going to fly all the way there to sit in the stands. I began to push my way through the muggy crowd down to the field. I got down there and found an open spot for myself. I sat down and let out a sigh of relief. "I did it. I made it here." But after that thought, another quickly followed, "Well, now what?" I had been ignoring this question ever since first hearing about this event. I still didn't know why I even felt compelled to go there in the first place!

As I looked around, I began to feel a bit awkward. Everyone around me was worshipping Jesus with such zeal and passion. They were pouring their hearts out. I didn't feel any of that. My entire relationship with God was still predicated on endlessly apologizing for my mistakes. And since I always felt overwhelming shame after apologizing, it had been months since I even initiated one of those conversations with God. I just sat there and didn't know what else to do. I really didn't want to have the same old conversation with God that I always did, but then I thought to myself, "You know what? I came all this way; I might as well try it one last time. What do I have to lose?" And with that, I got down on my knees just like I had so many times before, and started to apologize for all of my sins. But this time, instead of guilt and shame, something else started to take place.

As I began to apologize, I started to feel a sensation deep within my heart. It was like my heart was getting hotter in the midst of my chest. The feeling kept building and building and building. I started screaming in my head, "What is happening? What is happening?!" It built up so much that I felt like I was about to explode. I grabbed my chest and let out an audible scream, but as soon as I did, I saw a random picture flash in my mind. It was of two floodgates that were holding back massive waters. The doors began to shake under the power that was pent up behind them. Instantly, the gates burst open, and the water raged out. As soon as I saw this, I began to weep uncontrollably. I couldn't stop. I wailed loudly in the midst of that enormous crowd. It was like the doors of my heart had been blown off the hinges by that torrential flood. I didn't care if anyone was around me. I didn't care if

I was making a scene. And even if I did, there was no way I could stop that uncontrollable flood.

After what felt like an eternity, I began to calm down and regain my composure. I noticed a massive puddle of sweat and tears had formed where my face had been on the ground. I hadn't cried in years, let alone ever experience anything like that; whatever that was! It felt like for the first time in a thousand empty prayers, I physically touched heaven. I'll never forget what I felt when I finally stood up. It was like I was lighter. Like a weight had been lifted right off of me. I felt - free. It was as if all that anguish and pain trapped in my heart had been flooded out into that puddle in front of me. I stood there looking around at the people still worshipping their hearts out. They were completely unaware of what had just taken place right next to them. I was at a loss for words. My mind was completely clear for the first time in, well, forever! All I could do was smile. Before kneeling down I was bound in such pain and sin, living a lifestyle that brought me nothing but shame, but when I stood up, I had been 100% transformed; set free. I knew at that moment that my life would never be the same. I consider this the moment that I got saved. I may have grown up in the church, been to countless worship services, and heard every Bible story, but on that day in the sweltering heat of Nashville, Tennessee, I met God face to face.

I had an interesting thought while I stood there contemplating my new found freedom. "If this is what one moment of God is like, what would a lifetime with Him be like?" I didn't realize at the time the impact this thought would have on me. I flew to Nashville to satisfy my curiosity, but in doing so, I awakened a lifestyle where the books of the bible weren't just stories anymore, they would become real. Little did I know, what I experienced on 7/07/07 would be just the first few steps into a brand new life. And with that, our journey begins.

CHAPTER 1

THE POWER OF GOD

Everything began to change for me after flying home from Nashville. I would often find myself daydreaming about God all day long. The things that interested me before started to lose their appeal quickly. I wanted to know more about this new *Person* that I discovered; I absolutely had to! I remember grabbing my Bible and reading through the book of Acts two times over the very first day. Which if you know me is a miracle in itself because I am not a huge fan of reading. Something marked me in Nashville, and I couldn't get away from it. I began to pray and ask the Lord what to do next. I felt in my heart that there was something just beyond that initial experience, but I couldn't place my finger on it. And then one night, I had a dream.

I found myself walking into a massive building. It was dark, and there were people everywhere. I didn't recognize anyone around me or the premises at all. But as I looked out across the people, I noticed a giant stage in front of the crowd. A few moments later, an Asian man walked out slowly onto the stage. When he reached the middle of the platform, he slowly turned towards my direction and pointed his finger right at me. Out of nowhere, he began to shout powerful declarations over my life, and as he did, I felt a surge of power rush over my entire body. I don't know how I knew it, but I knew it was God's presence. I had never felt God's presence before, but somehow in my heart, I instantly knew what it was. I began to vibrate and shake uncontrollably under that power. The presence became so intense that it actually knocked me on my back. It started to rush over my entire body like a river, and its current seemed to only get stronger as I laid there. Just when I thought I couldn't take anymore, I suddenly shot awake to find myself lying in my bed. I had never experienced anything like that, and for a few fleeting moments, I could still feel that presence even after waking up. It lasted for just a few seconds, but at the same time, it lingered just long enough for me to know that it was more than just a dream. I sat up in my bed, and the literal words out of my mouth were, "What was that?" As I said before, I don't know how I knew that it was God's presence that I was feeling in the dream. It was like an instinctual knowing within my heart. But as I processed what took place, there was one more thing my heart *knew* as well: this dream was an invitation for more.

Over the next few days and weeks, I began to experience a hunger for God like never before. I started to pray for hours every single day. I absolutely had to experience what I felt in that dream. There were times that I would worship for a solid 8 hours straight. It was like a part of me was missing after that dream. That hunger for His presence kept drawing me deeper and deeper into the word, into prayer, into worship, into the pursuit of Him. I knew in my heart that God wanted to encounter me in real life as He did in that dream. And the more I prayed about it, the more I could feel that encounter inching closer and closer to me. Then one day as I was praying, I felt the Lord say that the encounter would take place sometime in 2007. I was thrilled to hear that! I was told this in mid-July of 2007, so I was expecting for it to happen at the end of July or early August at the absolute latest. I woke up every single day with the same expectation, 'TODAY IS THE DAY!' Things would turn out *slightly* different than I expected.

Over the next few months, I began going to every Christian event that I could. If there was a Sunday service, I was there. If there was a Wednesday night prayer meeting, I was there. If there was a church bake sale, I was there but most likely for the food in that situation. I couldn't get enough of God. I even heard about a revival meeting that was taking place at a local church in town. They were apparently hosting a preacher from Africa who had seen unbelievable miracles. You better believe I went to that meeting.

During the service, the man shared about the most incredible encounters you could ever imagine. I could feel my hunger growing within me. At the end of the meeting, the preacher wanted to pray for every person in the room, and he wanted to do that by giving them each a hug. The entire church then lined up single file as the preacher gave everyone a hug one by one. I thought it was a sweet gesture on the preacher's part to want to pray for every person in the church, that is until I saw my dad get a hug from him. As soon as he hugged the preacher, my dad fell to the floor and started crying. I just stood there, looking at my dad weeping on the floor, and then back up to see the preacher's open arms waiting for me. I remember thinking to myself, "If that's what happened to my dad, what's gonna happen to me!?"

I approached the preacher, somewhat hesitantly, and gave him a hug. I waited there for a moment to see if anything would happen, but nothing did. He then let go of me and looked me in the eyes and softly asked one simple question, "What is your name?" I mumbled out my name in response. He smiled back at me and said, "I will tell the Lord your name tonight." Many times over the years I had heard the phrase, *the fear of the Lord*. My whole life I never had realized what that phrase meant, but at that moment, I completely understood it. It's hard to explain, but when he said those words to me, I honestly felt terrified inside. Not in a fearful way though, but rather in a way that shows you just how small you are compared to God. As if you were to barely catch a glimpse, for the briefest of moments, of just how big the expanding universe really is around you. I don't know how I knew it, but I knew in my heart that something was going to happen later that night.

After getting home from the meeting, my sister, Monica, asked me if I wanted to play some piano with her. For some reason, the only thing that I wanted at that moment was to be alone; to process what had taken place earlier that night. I agreed to hang out for a little bit, but it seemed that the longer I sat there, the more I could feel something drawing me away to be by myself. I eventually looked at the clock and saw that it was already midnight. I told her that I was too tired to play anymore and so I got up and went to bed. There was a deep longing in my heart that seemed to be growing as the night went on. I had to get away by myself. I sat down on my bed and put my hands out in front of me. I had no idea what I was doing. I just did what felt natural at that moment.

(You may have thought the things you've read so far in this book were stretching, but to be honest, we haven't even scratched the surface yet. It's at this moment in the book where I really want you to continue reading with an open heart and mind. Maybe you're a Christian who has never experienced or seen these things before. Or perhaps you aren't a believer at all and have never heard of God in this way. Regardless of where you are at, as you read the rest of this book, please listen to the heart behind what I'm saying. I am just sharing my experience. Everything that has ever happened to me has only brought me closer to Jesus Christ. So you can either choose to believe it or not, that choice is yours. But I know without a shadow of a doubt that whatever you read about in this book can happen for you as well. What God can do for one, He can do for another. And with that said, let's continue.)

I just sat there in the darkness, waiting for something to happen. And with my hands out in front of me, as if reaching out to grab ahold of something -- or someone, I began to feel what felt like a pillar of fire appear in front of me. I couldn't see anything with my eyes, but I could touch it physically with my hands. I started to move my hands back and forth through the fire. When my hands were outside of it, they would be cold, but when I placed my hands in the midst of it, they would be blazing hot. I had never experienced anything like this before. For some reason, I kept thinking about when Moses saw a pillar of fire in the book of Exodus. I had heard that story a million times before but never did I think that those things could happen today. Eventually, the fire faded away and I found myself sitting alone in the dark again. I laid down on my bed and gazed up towards the ceiling. I had a thousand questions running through my head, but as much as I wanted to unravel them all at once, the only words I could formulate were, "Wow, God, you *are* real. You *really* are."

The next morning, I came downstairs to get some breakfast when I overheard my dad and Monica having a conversation about the night before. My sister asked my dad, "Did you feel the earthquake last night?" My dad replied that he felt it and that his whole room was shaking. Monica said she felt the same thing and that it was right after she and I went to bed. I thought to myself, "That's weird. What are they talking about? I didn't feel any earthquake last night." My dad went on to say that he shot wide awake at 12:15 AM to see his chandelier shaking above his head. They both then looked over at me as if to say, "Well, did you feel it, too?" I was so confused as to how I could have missed an earthquake. I stood there with a puzzled look on my face, pouring my milk slowly into a nice bowl of cereal when out of nowhere it finally hit me. I didn't feel any earthquake because at the exact same moment I was experiencing that strange pillar of fire. I then thought to myself, "Could that really have made the entire house shake? I didn't feel any shaking at all." The *incredible* experience I had the night before had now crossed over to *unexplainable* in my mind. It left me with so much curiosity, so much hunger to know more about *who* God really is. It left me with countless questions; I loved it. I had no idea heaven could be that real. But as fascinating as this encounter was, I knew it wasn't what I had felt in my dream. I knew this was just a taste of what was to come. I could have settled for what I experienced that night, but instead, I thanked God and pressed forward for more.

The following months, I went to even more meetings, gatherings, conferences, events, etc. I still woke up every single day with that same expectation of 'TODAY IS THE DAY'. But as I came home from each of those meetings, I started to feel discouraged that the encounter hadn't happened yet. I kept trying to plan it all out in my head. "I'm gonna go to this next event, and then God is gonna encounter me like He did in that dream! And then my life is never going to be the same!" But meeting after meeting it wouldn't happen. And I could feel my heart begin to ache from the mounting hope deferred. Then one day, I decided to make a promise to myself, "I'm not gonna try and plan it out anymore. If God wants to do it, He can do it on His own time." A part of me had begun to question whether God was going to actually fulfill His promise to me at all. And for my sanity, it was easier to stop thinking about it because it only made my heart hurt when it didn't happen. I had all but given up on the promise when I finally hit December of that year. I made amends in my heart that I must have been wrong in the fact that God was going to encounter me that year like I *thought* He had said. But things would suddenly change when I decided to attend one last big meeting in the year of 2007. This event would take place on December 31, 2007. The very last day of the year.

The particular gathering was the farthest one since my trip to Nashville. It was in Kansas City, Missouri, and by this time, not even a plane ride could slow down my hunger for God. It was an event called the *One Thing* conference, which apparently was going to have thousands of people bringing in the new year with hours of worship. How could I ignore it! Without hesitating, I hopped on a plane with some friends and flew to Kansas City. I walked up the front doors of the venue, just like I had so many times to various meetings over the past few months, but when I stepped inside, I quickly realized that this time would be different. When I walked through those doors, something about the building seemed eerily familiar. I couldn't place my finger on it, but it was like I had been there before. It wasn't until I walked in and saw the massive crowd in front of the stage that it finally hit me. "This is the exact place from my dream." You would think at this point that I got super excited at the prospect of seeing my dream fulfilled, but as crazy as it sounds, I had been let down so many times before that I just ignored the possibility of it even happening. I had so burned myself out trying to make it happen on my own terms that I lost any desire to try to figure it all out. I instead joined the crowd at the front of the stage and began to worship the night away.

Around 8 PM, worship had ended and some speakers had come out on stage to share. There were a lot of speakers that I had never seen before. It had become quite normal within these settings for me to hear from people for the very first time because my hunger kept bringing me to so many brand new places. But as I sat there, I saw someone come out on stage whom I had definitely seen before, except it wasn't anyone that I had seen at any church, it was the same Asian man from my dream. I stood there speechless as he came out and grabbed the microphone. That man went by the name of Che Ahn. He slowly scanned the crowd and then asked one simple question to everyone standing there, "Who here is from California?" I instantly felt chills as I slowly raised my hand in the air. He then prompted everyone in the crowd who was around those people to lay hands on them in prayer. And before I knew it, I was surround by people praying for me, but as they prayed, a girl stepped in front of me and looked me right in the eyes and said, "You are a messenger to California." When she said those words to me, something interesting started to happen: My entire body began to shake.

My whole body from head to toe began to tremble and shake under the power of God. I vividly remember screaming in my head, "Oh my gosh, it's happening! It's happening!! It is HAPPENING!!!" And for some reason, my entire left side of my body started to feel very heavy, like it weighed a thousand pounds. I tried to fight it, but I quickly realized it was no use. I fell to the floor in a trembling heap as the shaking continued. People around me started shouting powerful declarations over my life, and as they did, every word brought on more power. It was at that moment that I could feel countless eyes staring at me in the midst of the crowd, but there wasn't an ounce of me that cared at all at that moment. They had no idea the number of hours I spent in prayer. They had no idea that God was fulfilling a promise that I held so dear to my heart. They had no idea what this moment meant to me. I had spent a lifetime hearing *about* God, but at this moment, I was standing *with* Him, and nothing or no one was going to make me cherish it any less.

I half expected the encounter to last about as long as it did in my dream; which was maybe a few minutes at best. And after about 5 minutes or so, I began to thank God for what He had done and the promise He fulfilled, but to my surprise, the trembling and shaking continued. 10 minutes went by -- then 15 minutes -- then 20. "Surely this will end soon." I thought to myself. 25 minutes went by -- then 40 -- then 50. "I can't believe this is still going!" I kept thinking. 1 hour went by -- an hour and a half – then 2 hours. By this time, God had so exceeded my expectations that I started to get physically tired. I couldn't believe the words that were about to come out of my mouth, but I had to say it, "Okay, God. You did your thing. I think we're good now." You would think God would have stopped right then and there. Nope. 3 hours – 4 hours – 5 hours.

By this time, I was utterly and absolutely exhausted, and it was time to leave. I was still shaking, and I couldn't walk on my own, so my friends had to carry me out. They dragged me through the crowd towards the exit. But as they did, a man stepped in front of us; I could only see his feet because I couldn't lift my head enough to see his face. Out of nowhere he began to shout, "More God! More God!! More God!!!" I remember my friends instantly screaming back, "Oh no! Don't pray anything more over him! They shouted that because anytime someone prayed over me, the shaking would intensify. And when the man said those words, I started to feel my whole body begin to get heavy again like before. Now, let me say something really quick. I am an extremely skinny person; I always have been. And the guys who were carrying me were much, much bigger and stronger than I was.

But when this random man said those words over me, my entire body became so heavy that two fully grown men couldn't hold me up. And we all fell to the ground together under that weight.

Eventually, my friends were able to get me back to our hotel later that night. They laid me down on my bed as I continued to shake under the power of God. 6 hours – 7 hours now, and at 7 hours it finally ended. I remember laying there feeling like a train had run me over. All those hours in prayer asking for the power of God to hit me. All that time spent praying for Him to show me how superior His strength was to mine. I had absolutely no idea what I was asking. God had eradicated any idea within my heart that He wasn't 100% real. For the rest of my life, no matter what happens, no matter what argument someone tries to bring my way, no one can ever convince me that God isn't real.

As I laid there, I tried to process what had just taken place. But as I started to relive in my mind what had happened that night, I suddenly began to feel that shaking return. I instantly shot up in my bed and forced myself to stop thinking about it, and when I did that, the shaking slowly faded away again. Honestly, for a moment, it genuinely scared me. I could feel my heart racing in my chest. Then, out of nowhere, I heard a soft whisper, "I'm *always* that close."

Looking back at that moment, you may think that hearing that whisper would cause me to be frightened, but God always knows just the *perfect* way to speak to our hearts. And in all honesty, for the first time since I got saved, I wanted to know Him more than just an *all-powerful God*, I wanted to know Him as a *Friend*.

CHAPTER 2

I AM GABRIEL

At this point in the story, it might be best to introduce myself properly. You're probably saying right about now, "Um, we know your name is Gabe. It says your name on the front of the book and the chapter is called 'I am Gabriel' for crying out loud." But, believe it or not, Gabriel isn't my first name, it's actually my middle name. My full name is Juan Gabriel Lopez, and I went by the name, Juan, for the first 19 years of my life. The funny thing is, I always hated my middle name with such passion. I don't know why but I never liked sharing it with people, and I rarely said it out loud. That is until just a few weeks before my baptism in September of 2007, where something unexpectedly began to change within me. For some reason, I woke up one day and randomly thought about my middle name, but instead of hatred, I actually liked the sound of it. I liked the sound of it so much that I kept saying it over and over again, but only in my head of course. And even though I started to sorta-kinda like it within my heart, I still didn't want to say the name, Gabriel, out loud. So I just ignored the feeling and made sure not to tell a single soul about this strange inner struggle. But as if things weren't already weird enough, they were about to get much weirder.

One of the things I couldn't wait to do after getting saved was to get baptized. It was the first thing I was planning on doing when I got home. At the time, I found myself on a trip to San Francisco,

California. After my Nashville trip, I had heard about a large group of people that were planning on driving through California to visit different churches along the way. I somehow managed to talk both of my sisters into going on this trip with me called the Summer of Love Tour. It didn't take much to convince me to join a group of strangers and spend the next three weeks sleeping in tents. I look back at this, and I can't for the life of me figure out how I was so easily onboard with it. I hate tents. I hate hiking. Why did I think this was a good idea? Being saved only a week may have had something to do with it. But before I could leave San Francisco to come home, a guy named Jordan approached me and asked if he could share something. He pulled me aside and said, "Hey, I know you don't know me, and this may sound random, but I feel like God is going to reveal to you the full meaning of your name." I didn't understand what that meant, but I thanked him and went on my way.

As I traveled home, I got a phone call from my mom. She also wanted to share something with me. She said, "Son, your father and I were talking about you today, and we began to randomly talk about your middle name. We started to ask each other why we gave you the middle name, Gabriel. You know, I don't know what this means, but I just feel like God is going to give you the full meaning of your name." I thought it was bizarre that twice in one day, two different people told me the exact same phrase, but I didn't know what it meant, so I just brushed it aside. But after that Nashville experience, I started to become more interested in seeing that prophetic word about film come to pass in my life than to hear anything else! I was convinced that God wanted me to immediately be a filmmaker for Jesus! I look back at this now, and I want to say to my younger self, "Hello! God is trying to talk to you about something else! Wake up!" I was pretty slow to get things back then. Thankfully, God is patient.

When I got back home from my trip, something peculiar began to take place. I started to think about my middle name nonstop. I would wake up thinking about it, go to bed thinking about it, every moment of the day it seemed to be at the forefront of my mind no matter how much I tried to ignore it. I didn't share anything about what was going on with anyone around me, I mean, I still hadn't even said the name 'Gabriel' out loud out of fear. I even remember waking up one day and checking my email, and when I looked at my profile name, I had this crazy urge to change it to 'Gabriel Lopez'. It freaked me out so much that I instantly closed the laptop. I didn't understand why I was thinking these strange thoughts. It never occurred to me that God was at work. Then the day of my baptism came.

I had been looking forward to this day for some time. Surrounded by my parents and two sisters, I slowly climbed into the cold pool. I was nervous but very excited for this moment. They all took turns praying for me. Then, in the end, my dad put his hand on my head and placed me under the water and then back out again. As I came out of the water, no one said a word, but I could feel my dad trembling for some reason. I could tell he wanted to say something, but he couldn't get it out. Then, under the fear of the Lord, my dad said with shaky words, "I feel like we are no longer supposed to call you Juan, but we are supposed to call you Gabriel from now on." The moment he said those words, everything instantly made sense. The two prophetic words about the fullness of my name and the constant thoughts about wanting to change it. I opened my eyes, and for the first time in years, I said the name 'Gabriel' out loud.

"Gabriel."

The very instant I said my name out loud I went into a vision. I saw a picture of a golden sword floating in the air, followed by the words, "You are my sword." I didn't know what to think. I knew it was God. And I couldn't believe who God used to tell me that. My dad, who I was personally named after and carried the same name, 'Juan.' I can only imagine what he felt in that moment to have to let that go and trust God. I just smiled and said, "Ok, God, that's my name now." My entire life I used to hate the name Gabriel. But when I came out of the water, it was like I wasn't that same person anymore. In that moment, it became a perfect fit.

It was strange to go by one name every single day for 19 straight years, to then suddenly go by a different name the next. I remember wondering how people would respond to having to call me by a different name. But when I told my best friend, Stephen, about my sudden name change, his response made me feel at peace. He said, "If that's what you want to be called, then that's who you are to me. You are now, Gabriel." Stephen never once called me Juan after that, not once. The people who truly matter in this life will always love you no matter what.

It's funny how things change over time. Now I absolutely love telling people my name. Mostly because when I say the name, Gabriel, I know the history behind the name. I feel what I felt that day in the pool surrounded by my family. I can still feel the cold drops of water falling off my face as I slowly looked up into the sky. Every time I say my name, I am reminded that God can change the hardest of hearts.

I think the reason it took me so long to connect with what God was doing was that I was so consumed with the prophetic word about film. After getting saved, it was like I had to relearn everything I knew about God. I assumed that since I got a word about film, that I was supposed to run hard after being a filmmaker for Jesus. But it seemed the more I ran towards it, the less God talked about it. And for the life of me, I couldn't figure out why He always was more interested in talking about who I was rather than what I did. I was so eager to change the world that I couldn't see the change in right front of me -- the full meaning behind my name; a name that not only my dad called me, but my Father in Heaven as well.

Gabriel means: God is my strength ~ God's abled bodied one ~ Hero of God

Juan means: God is gracious ~ God is merciful

The full meaning of my name: "God is my strength, for He has called and enabled me out of His endless grace and mercy to be nothing less than a Hero of God."

I would love to say that I quickly understood the lesson that God was trying to teach me, but it would be some years before I did. And my pursuit of being a filmmaker first and foremost would only prove to be more difficult.

CHAPTER 3

ONE-WAY TICKET TO REVIVAL

One of the best jobs I've ever had was when I worked the concession stand at a movie theater. I first started working there a few months after that crazy New Year's Eve encounter. I thought that the most practical way to grow in being a filmmaker was to surround myself with as many films as possible. So every day at work, I would eat all of the popcorn I could handle, drink endless soda on tap, and watch every movie that came out for free. I was living the life. I even started ministering to my coworkers and praying for random customers from time to time. God must have done an excellent job at keeping me hidden from my bosses whenever I decided to pray for customers because I never got caught once. It led to a lot of incredible moments with total strangers. Things were going well in life, and I started to feel like my relationship with God had begun to grow. But deep down, that itch for adventure began to stir again.

One day I was talking with God, and I found myself saying this prayer, "I think my faith isn't being stretched enough where I'm at. Life has become too easy. Lord, create situations where I have to trust you more." I've since learned that this prayer is a very dangerous prayer. That same night, I went to bed and had a dream. In the dream, I was standing with Jordan, the guy who prophesied about my name on the Summer of Love tour, and his older brother. They led me down a hallway and introduced me to four of their friends. We then gathered together in a group and started to pray. I could feel God's presence begin to emanate from within the circle. It became super thick when out of nowhere I suddenly woke up from the dream to my phone ringing. I looked to see who was calling me, and to my utter shock, it was Jordan from the dream. We had exchanged numbers after the tour, but I hadn't heard from him since then. It had been almost nine months to this point. I picked up the phone and nervously answered, "Uh, hello?" Jordan's voice blared back through the phone, "Bro! You gotta come to Florida with us. There is a revival happening there. We're leaving tomorrow! Can you come?" My first response was, "Um, hi to you too, Jordan."

I told him to slow down and explain what was going on. It was strange enough that I was literally just in the middle of having a dream that involved him, but now I was left with trying to decipher what he was talking about. He finally went on to explain that tons of people were getting supernaturally healed in Lakeland, Florida and that he and his friends were going. I immediately knew there was no possible way that I could just up and leave from California to Florida. It was summertime, and the big blockbuster movies were just coming out at the theater. No one at my job was getting any time off. It was easily the busiest time of the year. I told him that I wished I could go, but there was no way that I could. He then said that if I changed my mind that they would keep a spot open for me at their house. I replied, "*They?* How many of you are going?" He responded back, "It's me, my brother, and four other guys." I sat there stunned at his response. It was just like my dream.

One of the many reasons why I couldn't go to Florida was because there was no way I could get time off work during the busiest time of the year for movies. I kept trying to forget the phone call that I had earlier with Jordan but my mind kept going back to that dream. *What if I'm somehow supposed to go to Florida?* I went into my shift that day and thought about how I could approach my boss. But no matter how I tried to word it in my head, I couldn't seem to make the phrase, *'I want to go to a healing revival in Florida and I don't know when I'm getting back'* sound any less crazy than it already does. I asked my boss if I could speak to him, so he brought me into his office and sat me down. He stared at me for what felt like an eternity, waiting for me to speak. The more I thought about it, the more I felt like God wanted me to be just completely honest with my boss. I vividly remember saying to God in my head, "Uh, are you sure about this?" But I knew in my heart that it was the right thing to do. So, as reluctantly as humanly possible, I started to share with him my plan to go to Florida and attend this incredible healing revival.

I held nothing back, and I mean nothing. I told my boss that I had just enough money for a one-way ticket to Florida and that I would have to leave during the busiest time of the year. I even told him about the dream I had the night before about my friends who were already going. I was sure he was going to think I was insane. After sharing everything, he just sat there quietly in his chair, staring at me. All I could do was wait for him to respond. I wasn't going to say anything else, I certainly had said enough already. He then finally opened his mouth and said, "So you're telling me, you want to just leave immediately for Florida on a one-way ticket?" I replied, "Uh, yes that's right." He continued, "And you have no idea when you are coming back? Or how you're coming back for that matter?" I replied back again, "Uh, yes that is also correct." It got quiet again, real quiet. I could tell this was all going just great. He then went on to say, "You know, if someone is gone for longer than two weeks we have to fire them legally?" I didn't respond that time. I instead chose to stare blankly at him. He then let out a big sigh and said, "But, I guess if you were gone for longer than two weeks I could just hire you back." I could feel my face trying to hide the obvious confusion. I couldn't tell where he was going with this. He then stood up and walked over to me and said, "Go to Florida. Don't worry about anything here. And if you're gone for longer than two weeks, I will just hire you back immediately. Go." I was stunned. I didn't want to push my luck so I thanked him and immediately left his office as fast as I could. As I drove home that day, I couldn't believe all that had taken place in such a short amount of time. God moved mountains like they were nothing. And before I knew it, I was on a one-way ticket to Florida.

I arrived at the Lakeland airport the very next day. Jordan and all the guys came to pick me up along the way, and we drove straight to the meeting. That first night was electric. I had never seen a line of people waiting to get into a church before. People were so hungry that they had been waiting there all day long to get a seat once it opened. At 7 PM, the doors burst open, and people ran down the aisles looking for open pews like they were Black Friday sales. I ran past elderly people, small children, moms, I didn't care, I wanted a good seat! We secured a section for ourselves and waited for the meeting to start. Once it did, things got even crazier. People were getting healed left and right. Casts were coming off, and crutches were left behind, it was happening so fast that I couldn't keep up. I had never seen anything like it. It was insane. After the meeting, we went out to eat as a group to process what had just happened. But after paying for my meal, I quickly realized that I had no more money left. I barely had enough money to get me to Florida, so after that meal, it was all gone. I instantly remembered the words I prayed just a few days earlier, *"I think my faith isn't being stretched enough where I'm at. Life has become too easy. Lord, create situations where I have to trust you more."* I had no idea at the time what I was saying. And before I knew it, I was on a one-way flight to Florida with no money to eat or and no way to get back. But if there's one thing that I've discovered about God in these particular moments, it's that all you can do is smile and welcome the adventure of a lifetime.

The next day we decided to get some lunch together as a group before the evening meeting. I walked into the restaurant with no money in my pockets and a belly full of hunger. I had never been in a situation before where I had to trust God like that. I didn't know quite what to do. As I stood there, I began to contemplate the reality that I may not be eating lunch, but in the midst of thinking that, a random stranger walked up to me and said, "Excuse me, I want you to have this." And he shoved something into my hand and quickly walked away. I opened my hand to find that he had given me a $20 bill. But the man had left so fast that I never even got a chance to thank him. I was blown away that God would bring me a random stranger to pay for my lunch. And over the next few days, this would become a regular occurrence.

Every time we went out for a meal, a total stranger would come up to me and pay for my food. I never knew who they were and it was never the same person twice. There was even one night where I opened my Bible at one of the meetings to find a $20 bill hiding inside. Every time I was given money, it was never a huge amount, it was always just enough to pay for my next meal. It was my daily bread. After about a week or so of seeing God come through like this, my faith had gone to a whole new level. One night, we were out late again after an unbelievable meeting. Not many places were open that late so we decided to go to a restaurant that served pancakes 24 hours a day. But as we sat down, I noticed that Jordan and his brother were rather quiet. I asked them what was wrong and they informed me that they didn't have any money left and therefore couldn't order food. I told them not to worry and that it was all on me. They shouted back, "But you don't have any money either!" I explained that everything would be okay and that we should just order in faith. Looking back at this moment, it's crazy to think that they actually took my advice. And without any of us having a single dollar to our name, we ordered as many pancakes as you could imagine. I even ordered a large glass of milk to wash down my delicious strawberries and whipped cream pancakes. After our meal, we sat there stuffed to the brim, drowning from the sea of pancakes. And just like clockwork, the waiter approached me to inform us that someone had just covered our dinner; at 3 AM mind you. It got to the point where I knew, without a shadow of a doubt, that God would provide for me. The next day as we drove to the meeting, something interesting began to happen along the way. Because we had so many guys with us, Jordan and I had to always lie down in the back of the truck just to fit everyone. And as we were driving down the freeway, I was thinking about all that had happened that week and how faithful God had been, but as I thought that, something caught my eye. Just above the truck, I started to see what looked like a cloud of golden sparkles appear out of thin air. It was small at first, but then it began to grow bigger and bigger; until it seemed to envelop the whole car. I stuck my hand out into the cloud and swished it around back and forth. Jordan noticed this and asked me, "What are you doing?" I laughed and said back, "What do you mean, 'What am I doing,' I want to see if I can touch it!" He sat there quiet for a second and then replied, "Touch what?" I was genuinely confused by his question. I looked at him and said, "What are you talking about? Can't you see this cloud thing all around us?!" He glanced back up towards the sky, surveying the surroundings with his eyes, and then said, "I don't see anything." I was shocked. I thought to myself, "How can I see this, but he can't?" I didn't know it at the time but what I saw around the car was a glory cloud. A glory cloud is a visible cloud of God's presence. I didn't know why I could see it and Jordan couldn't. All I know is that I will never forget it.

After the meeting, we found ourselves once again at a late night restaurant. I had been given $13 by a stranger so I was looking over the menu to see what I could afford. I was sitting across the table from a guy that was staying with us; his name was Kris Kildosher. The waitress approached our table and asked if we were ready to make an order, but as she said that, Kris looked up at her and said, "You try and read people's auras, don't you?" I was shocked. I sat there with my mouth hung open, avoiding eye contact with the waitress. She looked back at Kris and said, "Um, no, I don't do that." I could feel my face starting to get hot. I had no idea why he randomly said that out of nowhere! But Kris just kept his gaze fixed on her and didn't say a word; as if waiting for the right answer. She then went on to say, "Well, I don't do that anymore." Kris then finally spoke up, "You also have asthma don't you.

God wants to heal you of that." The waitress gasped and said, "How do you know all this?" Kris then got up from the table and began to pray for the waitress right there in the restaurant. My mouth was still hung open from his initial response, but now I was more shocked at what had transpired. The waitress ended up giving her life to Jesus after she got totally healed.

After our waitress had just casually given her life to Jesus, we put in an order of food. When she left, I quickly asked Kris, "What just happened? How did you know all that stuff about her?" He replied back, "It was a word of knowledge. God can speak to you details about people's lives if you let Him." I had never heard of anything like that before. "Where did you learn how to do that?" I asked. He took a drink of water as if this was normal everyday life and answered, "I go to Bethel Church in Redding, California. They have a ministry school there." I had never heard of Bethel before, but it wouldn't be the last time.

I had been in Florida for almost two weeks now. I had seen healing miracles, financial provision, and visible clouds of God's presence. This trip had far surpassed any expectation that I held, but there was one question still lingering in my mind: "How the heck am I gonna get home??" On the 13th day of the trip, I happened to wake up early at 5 AM suddenly. I was just about to try and fall back asleep when I felt the Lord say to check my bank account. I groggily reached over to my phone and typed in my bank details as I squinted at the bright screen. But when I saw what was in my account, my eyes shot wide open. There had been a deposit made into my account from my job for $500. I had no idea how that money got given to me. I hadn't been working because I was gone and even the checks that I usually received were never that large because I only made minimum wage. Still to this day I have no idea how I randomly got given $500. But as fate would have it, it was just enough to buy a return ticket home.

I was gone for exactly two weeks to the day; so I was able to keep my job without having to get re-hired back on. I couldn't believe how much my life had changed in just 14 short days. My faith had grown to whole new heights. But on that trip to Florida, something else had taken place as well: A tiny seed had been planted within my heart, a seed that started to grow. I thought often about what Kris had said that night at the restaurant. And I began to daydream about one-day visiting this fascinating new place called *Bethel Church*.

But little did I know, I would find myself there sooner than I thought.

CHAPTER 4

ON THE FENCE

Shortly after returning home from Lakeland, Florida, I heard about a one night only event that was taking place in town. Apparently, there was going to be some phenomenal speakers there that people were really excited for. The speakers were Shara Pradhan, Jill Austen, and some lady named Heidi Baker. I had never heard any of their names before so I didn't know what to expect; I wasn't disappointed.

I couldn't believe how anointed these speakers were. As they preached, whole sections of the room would start to weep under the presence of God. People were rushing the front and falling to their faces in desperation for more of Jesus. I had never seen anything like it. As soon as the meeting finished, my sister leaned over and told me that she's actually met Shara before. My eyes opened wide, "You know her? Can you see if she would pray for me?" I asked immediately. I could tell my sister regretted telling me that because she knew I wouldn't stop asking until she got Shara to pray for me. So at the end of the meeting, my sister brought me to the front and introduced me to Shara. I shook her hand and asked her if she would pray a blessing over me. I was expecting a gentle and sweet prayer to end the night. The prayer that I ended up getting was anything but that.

Shara laid her hand on my head and stood in front of me in complete silence. I closed my eyes and waited for her to say something, but after about a minute or two, I began to wonder why she hadn't started praying. I opened my eyes to see if maybe Shara had been distracted in some sort of way, but she hadn't, she just stood there -- motionless. About 5 minutes passed, and Shara still hadn't spoken a word to me. I was just about to open my mouth and say, "Well, thanks for that, I think I'm gonna get going now." But right before I could, a massive gust of wind hit me in the side of the face. It was so strong that it literally knocked my head to the side and I stumbled back. And as soon as it hit me, Shara shouted at the top of her lungs, "Whoa!" And with that, a prophetic word burst open out of her mouth like an explosion. "Bethel! The Lord is calling you to Bethel! I don't know what that means or what Bethel is but God says you have the DNA of Bethel. You are called there!" I couldn't believe what I was hearing.

After thanking Shara for changing my life, my sister peeled me off the floor and helped me to the car. The very moment that I got home from the meeting, I started to research about Bethel's ministry school. It turned out that their new school year was just beginning the following month. I applied without hesitation. I didn't understand how Bethel was going to play a part into my film career but I knew God was calling me there. And I didn't care that it was close to the starting date or if registration had possibly ended or not; I knew I was getting in. And sure enough, just ten days after applying, I had been accepted into the 2008 class of the Bethel School of Supernatural Ministry (BSSM). And within four days after getting accepted, I moved to Redding, California.

I was definitely nervous about moving to a new place that I knew very little about, and on what felt like a whim as well. But I knew in my heart that God was calling me to Bethel, and nothing was going to stop me. I moved into an apartment right across the street from Bethel, which was nice because I didn't own a car at the time. My roommates were extremely nice, and it turned out they were just as passionate as me. It was amazing to hear their stories of how the Lord drew them to Bethel. We all came from different walks of life, but at the same time, we shared one common mindset, *'I want to see Heaven on Earth.'*

A few days after arriving in Redding, my roommates and I decided to explore the city together. We had heard there was a local waterfall nearby called Burney Falls. The drive to the waterfall was beautiful; it was my first time living in a place that had mountains and lakes. But what I thought was going to be just a regular outing, turned out to be much more than that.

I was sitting in the backseat of the car looking out the window when I saw a random vision flash in my mind. I had been getting more and more visions as of late, and they were always exciting when they happened. The vision was of me standing in the forest on a dirt path. But just ahead of me, the path broke off into two separate directions. The path on the left went straight forward, but the path on the right had a wooden railing that went higher up into the forest. But as I drew my eyes to the top of the path on the right, I saw an angel calling me up there. That's when I instantly came out of the vision.

A few minutes later we arrived at the falls and started to walk around. We hung out at the waterfall for a while and then went on a hike around the area. As we were walking through the forest, we found ourselves on a dirt path. I looked up ahead and noticed that it broke off into two separate directions. I stopped in my tracks and freaked out for a second. The path on the left went straight ahead, and sure enough, the path on the right had a wooden railing that went higher up into the forest. The forest, the dirt path, the wooden railing, even the angle of which I was standing there looking at everything, it was all EXACTLY how I had seen earlier in my vision down to the tiniest detail.

But as I stood there in shock, I quickly noticed that my roommates were walking on the path going straight ahead. For a moment, I didn't know what to do, but my curiosity quickly took over. I yelled out, "Hold on!" As I ran up the path to the right. They looked back and screamed, "Where are you going??" -- "I gotta see something!" I yelled back as I sprinted up the path.

In the vision, I saw an angel pointing to something at the top, so I was super curious as to what was up there. When I got to the top, I looked around, and my eyes were drawn to something written on the wooden railing. Written in white chalk were the words, *"I love you."* I remember staring at the wooden post for a while just taking it all in. A few moments later, my friends followed me up the path to see what I was doing. But for those few seconds by myself, it seemed like time stood still. I thought because I had seen such a clear vision earlier that maybe God was going to reveal some big revelation to me. I was blown away that He would go to such lengths to express something so simple as love. I learned something new about the heart of God that day: No matter how subtle or profound an encounter may be, God's only agenda will always be love.

As we drove back home from the waterfall, I found my expectations towards BSSM beginning to change. I had come there to learn how to prophesy and heal the sick, and while I still wanted to do those things, for the first time I considered a different possibility: *maybe God brought me there to be His friend.*

CHAPTER 5

THE STREETS OF MEXICO

That first year at Bethel was unlike anything I had ever seen before. I was surrounded by hundreds of people who were on fire for God. We would worship for hours on end and take every opportunity to practice prophesying over each other. I started to understand how in coming to a place like this that my friend Kris had become so prophetic. Everyone around me was so hungry to learn and grow that it only spurred me on even more. But it seemed that in the midst of growing in my relationship with God and the gifts of the spirit, my desire for film was slowly beginning to die.

Ever since I got that prophetic word about film, all I did was try to make it come to pass on my own. I got that job at the movie theater, worked on various short films, and even practiced making my own videos whenever I could. But as hard as I tried to make it work, it never seemed to be in the conversation that God was having over my life. I was trying to force the agenda of film, but God kept opening doors to get to know Him more. And in the first few months of being at Bethel, after trying to force my own narrative in life, I got completely burned out on the idea of ever doing film again. I didn't care about the prophetic word anymore. I didn't want to change the world. I didn't want any of it. I was so confused at why God had ever said anything to me about film in the first place. I was convinced that film was NOT on the heart of God for me. The hardest part was this though: if I wasn't The Filmmaker, *who* was I? Little did I know, this was the start of something beautiful.

It didn't take me long to start growing in the gifts of the spirit after that. Now that I had given up the pursuit of film, I was able to devote all of my time to growing more *anointed*. Every day that I went to school, I would practice prophesying over anyone around me. If I met someone for the first time, I would give them a prophetic word. If I went to a birthday party, I prophesied over the birthday person AND everyone else at the party. I didn't know it at the time, but my pursuit of being THE FILMMAKER had transformed into wanting to be THE PROPHET. It was a personal goal of mine to become so gifted, that people would be awe inspired when they met me. And on my BSSM mission trip to Mexico, I would finally achieve that goal.

Every year Bethel has teams go out all over the world for mission trips. I had never been on an official mission trip before, so I couldn't be more excited at the possibility of seeing God move in the nations. I had been accepted to go to Mexico City, and low and behold; I found out that my friend Kris Kildosher was going as well. He was in his 2nd year of the school of ministry at the time. The healings and encounters we had witnessed together in Florida were the most incredible things I had ever seen in my life, but to be honest, they would be nothing compared to Mexico City.

As we arrived in Mexico, the team was separated into different host homes across the city. Every host home had a designated translator assigned to the house to help communicate with our host family; every host home but *mine* that is. The church we came to serve, saw that my last name was *Lopez*, and they assumed I knew Spanish, which I don't, so they didn't assign us a translator. It was myself and a guy named, Paul, from New Zealand, staying there at the home. So since I knew zero Spanish, and Paul-from-New-Zealand knew even less than zero, communicating about anything was interesting to say the least. I miss those late night conversations, "HOW DO YOU WORK THE SHOWER TEMPERATURE!?"

The healings that took place that week were unlike anything I had ever seen before. Every single meeting, we saw blind eyes open, tumors fall off, and people get up out of wheelchairs. Even when we evangelized in the streets, people seemed to be getting healed in droves. One day, we were driving on the bus on our way to another meeting when we had to stop for gas. As I waited for the driver to put gas in the bus, I closed my eyes and saw something unusual. When my eyes were open, I couldn't see anything in front of me, but when I closed my eyes, I could see the word, "*Cielo*" floating above my head. It was like a strange vision but only in my mind. I leaned over to one of the translators that was sitting across from me and asked her if the word *Cielo* meant anything in Spanish. She smiled and said, "Yes, of course. It means heaven."

I didn't know why I saw the word, heaven, but I thought maybe I should get off the bus and find someone to pray for. So I grabbed the translator, and we decided to check out the gas station. I noticed a man was standing inside by himself, I approached him and asked if he needed prayer for anything. He pointed to his stomach and said he had a tumor. I asked him if I could pray for it; he agreed. I placed my hand on his stomach and felt the tumor under his shirt. It was about the size of a baseball. As I started to pray, I began to feel waves of heat under my hand. I glanced up and noticed the man was feeling it as well. I said to him, "We declare that this tumor would completely disappear in Jesus name." Immediately, the tumor popped like a balloon. The man let out a loud gasp, "Gahhh!" I quickly withdrew my hand back out of shock. It happened so fast that I thought I hurt him in some way. He started running his hand over his shirt feeling for his tumor, but it was completely gone. Tears filled his eyes, and without hesitation, he leaned in and hugged us tightly. A few minutes later, the bus was ready, and we had to leave. As we drove away, I was trying to process what had just happened. The whole week was like that; nonstop heavenly encounters seemed to be waiting around every corner. But the following day, there awaited an encounter that would reveal to me the lesson that God had been trying to teach me for years.

We were walking in the streets doing evangelism when we came across an older lady on her way to the store. When I saw her, I felt the Lord say that she had hearing problems. We approached her and asked through the translator if she had any hearing loss. She nodded and said that she was almost completely deaf in her left ear. I considered laying my hand on her ear and praying for healing, but I had already seen deaf ears healed that week, I wanted to raise the stakes. I told her that I was going to walk by her and that my shadow was going to pass over her ear, and when it did, her ear would pop open. The lady seemed a bit confused that a random stranger was saying this to her on the street, but that didn't stop her from shrugging in compliance, as if to say, "Alright, Weirdo. What have I got to lose?" So I took a few steps back and slowly walked towards her. It was about noon, so I had to walk pretty close to her for my *shadow* to pass over her head, which I'm sure made things seem much less weird. But as soon as my shadow passed over her, her ear was 100% healed. The lady stood there in amazement, as well as the translator and a few other people who were watching. The lady ended up giving her life to Jesus and walked away from that moment with total hearing in both ears. As we walked home, I had an overwhelming feeling of accomplishment come over me, but for some reason, it didn't sit well with me. I don't know how to explain it, but when I felt that satisfaction after seeing that healing, I had a serious check in my heart.

I laid wide awake that night trying to figure out what was going on with me. I kept asking God what this feeling was in my heart, but I didn't hear anything back. I couldn't ignore it; I had to know why

I felt so unsettled. I laid there asking over and over and over again. I eventually tired myself out, forcing me to sit in complete silence. When I got quiet, I started to hear a phrase repeat itself in my head. "If I manage to see this healing, I will finally have something to show other people that will always impress them. And they will accept me because of it." My eyes widened. I sat up in my bed and looked out into the dark room. I realized that phrase I heard came from within the depths of my heart. I knew then that my pursuit to grow more in spiritual gifts was only to make myself more likable to others. I then heard God's voice, *"You are living in performance, and you have sacrificed intimacy."* I was stunned. I didn't respond right away, but eventually muttered out, "But, but, that doesn't make any sense, God. How can I see all of these miracles if I'm not walking in intimacy?" Immediately, the scripture, Romans 11:29, popped into my head. I couldn't recall what that verse said, so I opened up my bible and read it out loud:

"For the gifts and the calling of God are irrevocable."

When I read that scripture out loud, I heard God say to me, *"Just because you walk in gifts, doesn't mean you walk in intimacy."* I had no idea. I was judging my *intimacy* with God on the fact that I saw miracles, it hadn't dawned on me that it was because of an irrevocable gift. I began to ponder my relationship with God over the last couple of years. I started to notice that I always tried to be *someone* for God (the filmmaker, the prophet) but God always brought it back to simple intimacy with Him. I was terrified to let go of those aspirations. I thought being a filmmaker, and now a prophet, were the most impressive things I could become. I had no idea He always saw me as something so much more than all those things. He saw me as a *son*.

I repented for sacrificing my relationship with God in my pursuit to become someone amazing. And when I finally chose to give up those aspirations, I found myself in a conversation that God had been wanting to have since the day I got saved.

"Who am I?"

Now that we were finally on the same page, God would answer this question loud and clear.

CHAPTER 6

THE EYES OF JESUS

My life had begun to transform during my first year at Bethel. I had been on a journey for so long to pursue my own desires, that I hadn't taken the time to actually get to know the *heart* of Jesus. But after Mexico City, I started to sit with the Lord for hours on end and just talk with Him. It was hard for me to come to terms with the reality that God wanted me for *who* I was and not what I could do *for* Him. In my mind, I could grasp the concept of that truth; it just didn't make any sense to my heart. But during my second year at Bethel, that revelation would make the journey from my head to my heart.

A group of friends and I were driving down to a meeting we had heard about in Santa Cruz, California. There was a ministry there holding nightly Glory Meetings; I had to check it out for myself. At the meeting, I listened as the speaker started to share their testimony. They talked about the incredible miracles they had seen and what Jesus had done in their life. Everything they shared was excellent, but when they mentioned the name of Jesus, something within me jumped. I didn't want to hear about the miracles. I didn't want to hear about the prophecies, all I wanted to hear more about was this man named Jesus. It's not that I don't love miracles and the prophetic, obviously I did, it's just in that moment when he mentioned the name of *Jesus*, something was gripped in my heart by the beauty of God. I sat up in my chair, leaning to the edge of my seat as if waiting in anticipation for what was about to happen. But right when my heart began to drink deep of that moment, the speaker then changed the subject and segued into a different story. I felt like someone had stolen something from me. I had never felt that before. I was completely lovesick in that moment.

On the way home, my friends wanted to stop at In-N-Out to get dinner, but for some reason, I couldn't shake this feeling in my heart. I told them I wasn't hungry and that I wanted to wait by myself in the car. Which if you know me, turning down In-N-Out was the biggest shocker of the night so far. After they had gone inside, I began to ask God what was going on with me. I felt like I was grieving about what had happened that night in the meeting. I had never *longed* for Jesus like that before. I could feel something stirring deep within my heart, like tiny tremors before a volcano is about to erupt. From the core of my being, I could feel it rising up.

Out of nowhere, I got the sudden urge to scream in tongues as loud as I could. I had never done anything like that before, but it was like the tongues were bubbling up from deep within my soul. It felt like an itch that needed to be scratched at any cost. I had to let it out. But right before I could unleash that inner blast of tongues, a car of teenagers pulled up right next me. I noticed that my window next to me was wide open. I was forced to make a split second decision. Do I wait for the teenagers to get out of the car and leave, or do I allow this feeling to happen? Everything in me wanted to wait for them to leave, but I knew that this window of opportunity might close if I waited too long. A thought slowly made its way across my mind, "They're gonna think I'm crazy." But before I could allow myself to go any further down that path, I closed my eyes, gripped the chair under me, and started shouting in tongues as loud and as hard as I possibly could. The once bustling car of teenagers became quiet after that; very, very quiet.

I sat there for a moment, just listening to the thick silence around me. You would think that I was still waiting for the teenagers to leave, but to my surprise, I started to feel something that quickly made me forget they were even there. God's presence began to pour over me in that car like warm honey. The only way I can describe it is that it felt like *liquid* love. It was everything that I was yearning for earlier in that meeting. I had never experienced anything like that. In Nashville, I experienced the redemption of God. In Kansas City, I experienced the power of God. And in Lakeland, I experienced the faithfulness of God. But at that moment, I experienced the overwhelming *love* of God, and it was more powerful than all the other moments combined.

I had never felt anything like this before. My soul couldn't stop drinking from that well of love, quenching a thirst that I never knew I had. Suddenly, I felt that waterfall of his presence begin to move. It shifted away from me to outside of the car. My eyes snapped open as the well of His presence had moved away. I looked around me, and the teenagers were nowhere to be seen. I had no idea how long I had been there, but I wasn't done experiencing that love. I got out of the car and ran through the parking lot like a madman looking for it. I look back at this moment, and it's crazy to think that love so marked me that nothing could stop me. I don't share this story often because not many people will understand.

It's funny, initially, there was such an inner battle of whether or not I was going to look silly in front of others, but after I experienced God's love, that thought didn't even enter my mind anymore. I sprinted through the In-N-Out parking lot desperately seeking out the presence of God. I can't really explain how I even knew where He was or what I was looking for; I just knew I would know when I found it. I burst through the bushes to find myself in front of a nearby restaurant, and when I did, I finally found that presence. I can't describe to you how happy I was. It felt like I had won the jackpot. I laid down right then and there on the cement, under that waterfall of glory; as waves of His presence washed over me. At that moment, it's like God and I were the only people in existence. Some people may not understand that level of desperation. Only those that have experienced the radical love of God will get it. I can't explain it any clearer than that.

Little did I know, that my friends had returned to the car to find my door wide open and me completely gone. They started calling out to me, but I couldn't hear them. I was *lost* in God's presence. Fully consumed. They eventually made their way through the bushes to find me lying on the floor of a different parking lot. Two of my friends approached me and tried to help me up, but as soon as they touched me, they both fell out under the presence of God. Now God had claimed three victims.

We laid there in the freezing cold for about 30 minutes. I didn't notice the cold though, I barely even noticed my friends. I was happy spending the rest of my life there on that asphalt. But eventually, I heard one of them say that we should get back on the road because we still had a five-hour journey back to Redding. And with that, they managed to pick me up and drag me back to the car. But when they moved me from that spot, they moved me out from under that waterfall. I was so confused at what was happening. One moment, I was *consumed* by the love of God, and the next, I felt absolutely nothing. I realized that I couldn't move my legs as I tried to struggle free from their grip. I couldn't speak, I couldn't move, all I could do was scream in my head. "Why can't I feel it anymore!" The pain I felt in that moment was indescribable. Once I had experienced God's love, being removed from it was the worst hell I had ever felt. I began to wail at the top of my lungs. They picked me up and threw me in the backseat of the car. I couldn't control myself; I wept from the pain of not feeling that love anymore. It was like my soul had been ripped out from the depths of my being. And with that, we drove off into the night. All I could do was mutter out a faint whisper, "God, come back. Come back. Come back."

I felt like I had lost everything. It was the greatest feeling I had ever experienced, and it was taken away from me like it was nothing. I bled tears of intense pain at the thought of never seeing it ever again. But as I sat there in the backseat, I started to feel a warmth seep into the car. I opened my eyes and looked out into the dark car. My voice trembled, "God, is that you? Is that you?" The presence began to increase all around me slowly. It felt like I was breathing fresh air for the first time. I couldn't believe it returned. I started feeling that warm honey drip down into my soul to replace what I had lost. I closed my eyes and screamed at the top of my lungs, "YES!" And when I did that, I went into a vision. But this vision was unlike any I had ever experienced before. I could see everything around me as if my eyes were open. I looked around and saw my friends sitting in the car, I looked out and could even see the road we were driving on. I saw all of this with the same clarity that I can see with my eyes open, but my eyes were closed. I had no idea what was going on. I looked up at the roof of the car, and for some reason, I could completely see through it as if it were a moonroof. I gazed deeply into the night sky and all of the bright stars throughout. As I look back on this moment, 2 Corinthians 2:13 comes to mind, *"whether in the body or apart from the body I do not know, but God knows."* I had never been in a vision this clear before. I don't fully understand what happened to me, but God knows.

As I stared into the night sky through the closed roof of the car, I became enthralled by God's creation. It started to feel like I was barely in the car anymore; like I was somewhere else far away. I could see space, galaxies, stars, so many different things. His creation undid me, but as I stared into that vast expanse, I saw the most beautiful thing I have ever seen in my entire life. Suddenly, as I sat in awe of His creation, the eyes of Jesus appeared in front of me like a blazing fire.

I began to scream to myself in the backseat of the car. As incredible and vast as those galaxies and stars were, they paled in comparison to the eyes of Jesus. I was absolutely terrified by how majestic it was. Those eyes could see right through me. Deeply piercing. They embodied authority. After a few moments, those intense brown eyes slowly faded away into the background of space, but as quickly as they had left, they reappeared again as soft blue eyes. This time, His eyes carried so much peace. A peace that I can't describe. Then they faded away again, and then returned with a different color. Every time they changed, they would carry a different color, and therefore reveal a different part of God's heart. They just kept changing, and changing, and changing, until I eventually lost count of all the different colors within His eyes.

Next thing I know; I could feel a gentle tapping on my shoulder. I snapped out of it and noticed that the car had stopped and that they were all staring at me. I gave the girl that had been tapping on my shoulder a baffled look. She then pointed outside the car and said, "We're at your house." My confusion continued as I looked at her and said, "How's that possible? We've only been driving for like 20 minutes. We just left In-N-Out." She didn't respond right away, but then said with a soft voice, "Gabriel, we drove all the way home. That was five hours ago." I couldn't believe it. I had been staring into the eyes of Jesus for hours on end, even though it seemed only to be minutes at most. I had lost all track of time; like I had stepped into eternity for a mere moment. And with one step towards that beautiful place, everything outside of the love of God ceased to exist.

There are moments in our lives that we can look back on and see the true benchmarks of change. This experience marked me. Marked by the love of God. It would be years before I shared it with anyone and this book is the first time that I've ever written about it. I had only planned to tell my future wife about it and that was it. But the funny thing is, years later, my future wife would already know about this encounter. Oh, I forgot to mention, the girl that was with me in the car that night, her name was Louise -- my future wife.

CHAPTER 7

LOVE OF MY LIFE

I was sitting in class one day in BSSM when the speaker stood up and started to share a fascinating testimony. It was about a young girl, from Wales, who had felt the Lord tell her to go to Moriah Chapel and shout, "Wakey Wakey." Moriah Chapel was the birthplace of the Welsh Revival that took place in 1904. The young girl in the story was a seer, which in the bible it talks about seers being prophets that often see the Lord's voice, whether by interacting with angels or having visions. But when this young girl stood in front of Moriah Chapel and shouted, Wakey Wakey, she saw a massive angel wake up from in front of the church. She looked at the towering angel and asked, "Who are you?" The angel responded, "I am the angel of the 1904 revival, and you've just woken me up." She asked the angel why it had fallen asleep, and he replied, "Because the people had stopped calling out for revival." She then asked if he was going to be a part of a new revival coming to Wales, the angel laughed and said, "The angel that is bringing in the new revival is much bigger than I am."

I had never heard a testimony like that before, and to my surprise, the speaker went on to say that the girl who shouted, Wakey Wakey, was in our class. He pointed out to the audience and told her to stand up. I turned around, and in the seat sitting directly behind mine, stood up a young girl with long brown hair. When class ended, I turned around and decided to introduce myself. She told me her name was Louise, and that she was from Wales. I told her how cool her testimony was and that I wished I could see in the spirit like she could. She offered to pray for me if I wanted, so without hesitation, I stood up in front of her and held out my hands and closed my eyes, ready to receive. Her prayer started out just like any normal prayer, but I quickly noticed that she began to stutter and mess up her words constantly. I didn't really mind at first, but as the prayer went on, I could tell she became very nervous. Her words eventually trailed off, and it got really quiet. I didn't know if she was waiting on God or something, but when enough time had passed, I opened my eyes to discover that she was completely gone. She straight up left in the middle of praying. No amen, no see you around, no nothing. What I didn't know at the time, was that Louise actually had a crush on me. She had already liked me from afar, so before she could finish her prayer, she ran off because she was so nervous. I was left standing there looking around the room for answers, when I finally said to myself, "That girl is weird." It would be an entire year later before our paths would cross again.

I was now attending our annual school retreat to start my second year in BSSM. On the last night, we would always have a huge worship night to end it all. I was standing in the middle of the crowd, minding my own business, telling the Lord how grateful I was to be at Bethel, when out of nowhere God said to me, "You are going to know Louise Watkins." I was shocked. I hadn't thought about her since that awkward prayer a year before. I said to God, "Uh, that weird angel-girl, God?" I didn't hear any response, so I ignored it and went back to worship. The next day, I returned home from the retreat and was greeted by my new roommate. We had just met, so in the spirit of getting to know each other, he offered to buy me dinner at In-N-Out. I quickly answered, "Um, yeah! That sounds great, thanks. Will it just be us? Or is anyone else going, too?" He looked at me and said, "I invited a friend of mine to come as well. Her name is Louise Watkins. Do you know her?" It hadn't even been 24 hours since the Lord told me that I would know Louise, and before I knew it, we had picked her up and drove, in silence, to In-N-Out.

We finally sat down together at In-N-Out; I was really hungry, but I was far more interested to see where this whole thing was going. It was a bit awkward at first, considering that the last time we spoke, she had walked away in the middle of praying for me, but as the night progressed, my viewpoint on her began to change. She wasn't awkward anymore, and we were able to engage in deep conversation. It was a great *second* impression, and after that night, we started hanging out regularly. Though, I still wondered what the Lord entirely meant by saying I would know her. I thought it might have something to do with the fact that I had been praying for God to open my eyes more to see in the spirit, and that maybe Louise was going to play some part in helping me walk that out. I never considered that she would play a much more significant role in my life.

Every time we hung out, I would ask her tons of questions about angels and seeing in the spirit. I was fascinated by this gift that God had given her. I would always ask her, "What do you see over here? Do you see anything around me? What's happening in the service right now?" I was filled with a hunger to see in the spirit like she did. But as time went on, something strange began to take place. I started to notice an even greater gift within her that I hadn't seen before – her heart.

Our hangouts turned from talking about angels to talking about everyday life. And it's not that I didn't want to see in the spirit anymore, it was still a huge desire of mine, it's just the other aspects of her life began to sparkle even brighter. Her gift was incredible, but it paled in comparison to who she was as a person. I suddenly wondered if that's what God had been trying to teach me about myself this whole time. I was always pursuing a greater gift or an impressive title; I hadn't considered that there was an even greater treasure already within me. What God had been trying to tell me, began to play out right in front of me. The way I saw Louise, was the *exact* way God saw me, too. He didn't just love me for my gifts; He loved me for me. I finally realized that it didn't matter if I became the most powerful miracle worker in the history of the church, God was *more* interested in my heart.

After about a year of getting to know each other, Louise and I would eventually start dating and continue to build upon that beautiful foundation of friendship and discovery. She would become my closest friend in all of Redding. But there was someone else who was my closest friend in all the world. I haven't mentioned my best friend yet, because, unfortunately, that road leads to a dark place. But the story needs to be told. It must be told.

CHAPTER 8

GOODBYE, MY FRIEND

I have done my best to avoid talking about my best friend, Stephen, for as much as I could in this writing process. It's not that he wasn't present during my journey so far, he was actually there throughout it a lot, it just hurts to relive those past moments. I have never written about this story before; I've always stopped myself, and to be honest, with tears in my eyes right now, it still terrifies me. But before I unearth the pain, let's revisit the good.

I met Stephen Mariani for the first time in 1998. I was only ten years old at the time, and I had just moved to Victorville, California. My mom had landed a job there being the principal at Kingston Elementary. I remember being so nervous on the first day of school because everyone else had known each other for years. And having your mom be the principal of your school didn't make for the best of introductions. But as I sat there by myself, a young kid walked up to me and introduced himself. "Hi, I'm Stephen, what's your name?" He asked me. I quietly replied back, "My name is Juan. I'm new here." He cracked a smile and said, "Yeah, I know." We both laughed, and with that, Stephen took a seat next to me, and from that day forward we would become inseparable.

Because my mom was the principal of the school, we would have to get there very early every day and leave very late. I was always so bored after school because all the students had gone and there was no one to play with. But every chance that Stephen got, he would stay late with me after school just to hang out. I can't even begin to describe the mischief that we would get in. We had constant lightsaber battles with teacher's yardsticks, which always led to them snapping in half. Whenever we noticed that the vending machine in the teacher's lounge was freshly stocked with candy, we would sneak in and steal as many as we could carry. One story, in particular, comes to mind from when we raced each other with the nurse's wheelchairs, which resulted in the winner (me) losing control of the wheelchair and crashing it; breaking it into a thousand pieces. We fled the scene of the crime and were never caught; *sorry* mom, that was me. Those are some of the best memories I have in life. Even now, it brings a smile to my face that warms my soul.

As the years went on, Stephen and I only grew closer. We spent just about every weekend at each other's house. And even when I couldn't go over, we would often call each other on the phone and sync both of our TV's together so we could watch Aladdin at the same time. The syncing of our TV's would often take longer than the actual movie itself, but it was always worth it. Even on the days I was sick and had to stay home from school, Stephen would still find his way into my mom's office during lunchtime just to have a chat with her. Our lives were one and the same. Whatever popular trend was taking place at the time, we would master it together. We went through Pokemon cards, Dragonball Z, Star Wars, Lord of the Rings -- I could go on and on. Growing up with two older sisters, Stephen wasn't just like the brother that I never had; he was my brother.

When we got into high school, we started really getting into playing the popular Xbox game, HALO. We would have halo parties every weekend with all our friends and play late into the night. Out of all the people that would come to our Halo parties, there were four of us that were the best. It was myself, Stephen, Kevin, and Eric. We got so good at playing Halo together that we formed a team to play online and in tournaments. At one point, we were even sponsored by the energy drink, Vault. Every single night, and I mean every – single – night, the four of us would play Halo for hours on end until one of us eventually started yelling at another one for some random mistake, which always resulted in them getting so mad that they turned their Xbox off. That's how we knew it was probably time to go to bed. But as the next day came, it was like nothing ever happened. We weren't just teammates on a video game; we were the best of friends.

Even after getting saved a few years later and our Halo battles eventually dying down, the four of us still remained just as close. Stephen went off to college, Eric joined the Navy, I found myself at Bethel, and since Kevin was always smarter than all three of us combined, he went off and became a Radiologic Technologist and eventually a Cat Scan Technologist. (When I read his job title, I say to myself - *cat scan* - yeah, I know those words).

Even though there was now a physical distance between all of us, our hearts were still just as close. I would often call Stephen to tell him about my adventures at Bethel. He loved hearing about the crazy things God was doing. I remember one time, I had sent him some worship music in the mail and told him to listen to it. But when he turned it on, he began to weep for no reason. He said he could feel the presence of God just like I had been telling him. I can't describe to you the joy it brought me to talk with him about the love of God. Thinking back to that will always bring a smile to my face. Always. But as time moves forward, so must our story. Everything inside of me wants to stop writing this. I want to snap the pen and throw it away as if that would somehow make it all vanish. But I can't stop now; there is a story to be told. It needs to be told. A beautifully hard story. So with trembling hands, let's pick up that pen and continue.

One day, while in Redding, I was housesitting for a couple that was out of town for a week. They had a massive property in the mountains with over a hundred potted plants, two dogs, and seven cats. The oldest of the cats was 17 years old, and she required a particular medicine that had to be hidden in her tuna. She may have been ancient, but don't let that fool you, she would turn into Neo from the Matrix whenever she noticed me slip something into her food. It took me 6 hours every morning to take care of them all.

There was no cell phone reception anywhere on the property and Louise was back home in Wales at the time. I hadn't talked to anyone for days because I couldn't communicate with the outside world very much. That is until one day when I heard the phone ring in the house. I hadn't heard their house phone all week, so I hesitated as to whether I should answer it or not. I paused for a moment and then eventually decided to pick it up, "Hello, this is Gabriel speaking. Who is this?" My dad's voice came back through the phone, "Son, where have you been? I have been trying to reach you." I was shocked to hear my dad's voice. I replied back, "I don't have any cell phone reception where I'm at because I'm watching someone's house by myself in the mountains. How did you get this number anyway?". He went on to say, "That doesn't matter. I have something to tell you. I hate to be the one to tell you this, son. But, it's about Stephen." My heart immediately sank; I could tell my dad was struggling to find the words to speak. I screamed back, "What happened? Just tell me!" His voice quivered, "He was in a motorcycle accident, and, he died, son." I sat there on the phone, completely silent. I couldn't speak. I couldn't think. I didn't respond back at all. My dad's voice broke through the phone, "Did you hear me, son? Are you there?" After a few moments, I replied back, "Um, yeah, I'm still here." My dad was quiet, then asked again, "Son, do you understand what I'm saying to you right now?" I didn't respond the second time either. My dad took a deep breath and reiterated, "Son, I need to know if you understand what I'm saying. Stephen was in a motorcycle accident. And, unfortunately, he passed away." My voice began to tremble as I answered back, "I .. I hear you, Dad. I understand what you're saying." He continued, "I'm so sorry that I can't be with you right now. I'm so, so sorry." The only thing I could say in response was, "I understand. I need to go now. Ok?" I hung up and stood by the phone in complete silence. I was in utter shock.

When I hung up the phone, I stood there for a while trying to grasp the conversation that I just had. I don't know why I reacted like that. My mind couldn't wrap itself around the reality of what my dad had just told me. It was like I was staring at the hull of a sinking ship, hearing the deafening cracks throughout its wooden interior as the water slowly seeped through. I could feel the walls of my mind beginning to buckle under the pressure just like that frail ship. And before I could brace myself, the walls shattered under the weight of death. I fell to the floor in the kitchen. I immediately started hyperventilating. I couldn't see two feet in front of me from the flood of tears that gushed from my eyes. I just started screaming, "No! No! NO! This can't be happening! This can't be happening, God! Why God? Why?!" I wailed as loud and as hard as anyone has ever cried before in the history of man. I may have been surround by countless animals and plants, but at that moment, I felt so alone.

I cried myself to sleep that night, but when I finally managed to slip into unconsciousness, I found myself in a dream. In the dream, I saw two angels carrying someone over a wooded area. I looked closer and noticed that it was Stephen in their hands. He had just died, and the angels were carrying him off to Heaven. There was a crown on his head that looked like Christmas lights, and the look on his face was priceless. Next thing I know, I was in my room, and Stephen was sitting at the foot of my bed. I sat up and gave him the biggest hug. He started to apologize and explain how he had died. He formed his hand to look like a motorcycle and recreated the whole scene for me.

Even in his explanation of his own death, he still managed to make me laugh. I suddenly woke up from the dream and found myself alone in a dark room; my eyes still swollen shut from the crying. I wished seeing him hadn't been just a dream, and that him dying was the real nightmare, but as I laid back down, I knew what was true. I still felt so much pain and anguish inside, but that dream gave me a hope that I would have never had otherwise: the hope that my future with him will be longer and more glorious than my past ever was.

I woke up the next day with the unfortunate reality that the world hadn't stopped to wait for me. There were hungry animals and thirsty plants everywhere I looked. I was in the kitchen preparing the dog food when the two dogs started impatiently barking at me. At first, it didn't phase me, I had been walking around the house like a zombie; completely numb and silent to everything. But they started barking louder, and louder, and louder; to the point where I couldn't take it anymore. I spun around and threw my hands in the air in a fit of rage that I had never experienced before. And just as I was about to scream from the depths of my broken being, "SHUT --- UP!" I heard a faint voice, as soft as a whisper, say one simple word to me, "*Love.*" I stopped in my tracks, still shaking from the rage like a trembling gun in the hands of a madman. I held myself there, suspended in that moment, debating on whether or not to unleash the fury that had been building inside of me, but instead, I lowered my hands and let out a deep breath. I looked at those barking dogs and chose to love them instead, and with that, I turned around and finished preparing their food. Still, to this day, I have never had a moment in my life that was harder to choose love than that, and it was on two annoying dogs.

At first, I was deeply distraught that I was by myself during this hard time. Louise wasn't there, my family wasn't there, no one was there but a herd of animals and God. But as I look back on that time, I'm glad I was by myself. Every so often, I would be in the middle of watering a plant, when I would have to put down the pail of water and just cry for an hour straight. Then, when I had the strength, I would pick up the bucket and continue watering. I did that non-stop for an entire week. No one could hear me for miles, and because of that, I held nothing back.

I learned a lot about God during that week. Anytime I would break down in tears, I could feel His strong arms wrap around me and hold me close. I felt as if I was lying in the depths of the deepest and darkest canyon in all of existence, but to my surprise, God didn't send down anecdotes of comfort from a far-off throne, He climbed down there to the depths of my pain and wept right alongside me. July 16, 2010, was the hardest day of my life, but the week that ensued, revealed a part of God's heart that I had never seen before.

The road to healing after that was long and arduous. I had to seek out grief counselors and surrounded myself with family. And I pulled Kevin and Eric even closer than before. We all had lost a brother that day. And I knew no one in the world could understand my pain like they did. It wasn't until about a year later that I could even hear the name, Stephen, without bursting into tears. I had to wake up every morning and say, "God, help me through today." And every single day, He did just that. I constantly declared, "GOD IS GOOD!" Even if I didn't feel like it, especially when I had no idea why my best friend died at the young age of 22. And every so often, I could feel that tinge of pain begin to rise up within me, the why of it all, but every time I peered down that path, all I could see was a future of bitterness and hatred from that *why*. So I chose to put my faith in God and seek after His peace instead of my answers. The peace that surpassed my understanding, and protected me from myself. The literal manifestation of Philippians 4:7:

"And the peace of God, which surpasses all understanding, will guard your hearts and your minds in Christ Jesus."

I barely made it out of that season alive, and after many hours of counseling, long talks with family, and even longer talks with God, I started to feel joy return to my heart. But as I finally started to find my footing again in life, there would be something waiting for me in the shadows that would crush my legs for good. As much as I want to, I can't put down the pen just yet. We have another story that needs to be told, and it's not an easy one to share. Stay with me. We're almost through this.

CHAPTER 9

NEVER ALONE

The strange thing about death is that it feels like a million years ago and just like yesterday all at the same time. It had now been a year and a half since Stephen died. At the time, I was working a job doing home care for people who had disabilities; which meant I stayed overnight at the client's house for days at a time to take care of them. It was a stressful job, but I loved it. The previous year and a half had many ups and downs, but there were many positives just ahead on the horizon.

After Louise and I finished our last year of BSSM, she had to move back home to Wales because her visa was up. We were left with a decision to make: Either she goes, and we never see each other again, or we take our relationship to the next level. That was an easy choice. Shortly after finishing school, I flew to Wales and surprised Louise by proposing to her in her favorite castle. It took a lot of planning, a lot of money, and a lot of lying about where I was – but that last part was for a good cause! After returning home, we immediately began the fiancé visa process to bring her back over to America for good.

I'll never forget the day I told Kevin that Louise and I were getting married. He was busy becoming a super-smart Cat Scan Technologist, but he still somehow managed to find time to play Xbox Live with me. As soon as I heard Kevin's voice over the microphone, I yelled, "Bro! Guess what! I'M GETTING MARRIED!" He screamed back,

"What!? No way, dude! That's awesome! We're gonna have so much fun at your wedding!" It was always fun telling people that Louise and I were getting married, but there was something special about sharing it with a close friend. And if there's one thing I've learned about wedding planning it's this: enjoy those special moments. Planning a wedding can be stressful, learn to appreciate the little things. But do you know what's even more stressful than wedding planning? It's planning a wedding AND filing for a fiancé visa at the same time; all while your fiancé lives halfway around the world with an eight-hour time difference.

Trying to marry someone from another country is just like you see in the movies. You have to prove your relationship isn't fake. I had to send emails, text messages, pictures, dinner receipts, everything. I compiled 60 pages of evidence showing our relationship was genuine, and we were still denied the first time because they wanted more proof. The second time, I didn't take any chances, I sent in absolutely everything within the knowable universe pertaining to our relationship. I even got a signed certificate from a certified counselor in a pre-marital course. It resulted in over 100 pages of evidence proving our relationship. We were accepted that time. Things were starting to looking up after a long season of obstacles. It was like I could finally see the light at the end of the tunnel, but, then it happened, and everything went to black.

I was working one afternoon with a client when the Lord spoke to me out of nowhere. He said, *"In this life, the word alone does not exist, only the lie of its existence does. For there are those that define their lives off the word alone. Whether I'm talking about people who stand on the power of the bible or those that live under false realities, both are true."* It came through clear as a bell. I didn't know why God had told me that, I just knew it was important, so I pulled out my phone and jotted it down. I went about the rest of my day as usual after that. Later that night, I was on my way home from work when a text suddenly came through to my phone. I checked to see who it was, and to my surprise, it was my ex-girlfriend from high school. I hadn't talked to her in years, so I knew it had to be important. I opened my phone to read the text, all it said was: "Did something happen to Kevin?" When I read those words, it was like my stomach dropped below my feet. I instantly wanted to throw up. I scrambled to pull up Kevin's social media page as fast as I could. Right away, I started seeing comments like, *I will always love you, Kevin,* and *Rest in Peace.* That's when I noticed an article had been posted on Kevin's profile with his name on it. I clicked on the link, and the first line read, "Motorcyclist struck by car, killed." I couldn't read any further, I closed my phone and set it down next to me. I didn't cry or anything, I just went home, turned out the lights, and crawled into bed; afraid. I had never felt more alone in my entire life. I don't know why I didn't cry; it's like I became instantly numb to all feeling at that moment. I felt nothing, nothing but fear.

As I laid there in my bed, physically shaking from the fear, I suddenly felt something step into the room. I immediately knew it was bad, but not just bad, it was evil. I looked out into the dark room, half expecting to see the devil himself. I could feel a thick cloud of dread slowly filling the air around me. I had never experienced fear like that. It was suffocating. I laid there, paralyzed by it. Suddenly, it occurred to me that I now had more best friends in Heaven than I did on Earth. That realization killed me inside. I had never felt more alone, but then, out of the darkness, a voice spoke to me, *"I will be your best friend."*

For some reason, when I heard that voice, I was instantly reminded of what I had written in my phone earlier that day. I reached for my phone as fast as I could, it's bright light suddenly pierced through the dark room as I desperately fumbled around trying to find the words. That moment truly felt like life or death, like all of the oxygen was slowly being sucked out of the room, leaving only a few precious seconds left to live. I found the note from earlier and immediately started reading it out loud, "The word alone does not exist. It's a lie. I am not alone. I am not alone!" I kept reading it over and over again, only this time I started shouting it, "The word alone does not exist! It's a lie! I am not alone! I am not alone!" I could feel those words clashing against that cloud of fear that had its hands firmly around my throat. I shouted it even louder now, "THE WORD ALONE DOES NOT EXIST! IT'S A LIE! I AM NOT ALONE! I AM NOT ALONE! I – AM – NOT – ALONE!" I felt something snap in the room as if a window had been shattered right in front of me, forcing the cloud to disappear through its open cracks. I laid there on my bed, gasping for air as the room cleared, still whispering between breaths, "I am not alone. I am not alone. I am not alone."

The next morning, I woke up to an eerily quiet room. As I sat up in bed, exhausted from war, I still wondered why I hadn't cried yet. It was like my emotions had been completely shut off, and all that was left was the battle between *alone* and *not alone*. I reached for my phone to continue reading the note to myself. I had easily read it over a hundred times before I could fall asleep. But even after all of that, I couldn't stop reading it, it was all that I had. After declaring it a few more times, I decided to finish reading the article that had been posted on Kevin's profile. But even as I read through the details of the accident, I still felt numb inside. I wanted to cry so bad. But when I got to the end of the article, something caught my eye. It said that Kevin was in a head-on collision at exactly 4:22 PM. I set my phone down and thought to myself, "What time did I write that note yesterday?" And as I looked back at the timestamp in my phone, I let out an audible gasp; it was written at exactly 4:23 PM; one minute after the accident. It had taken me about a minute to write out the note God had told me. It was then that I realized that at the exact moment my best friend left the Earth, God spoke to my heart and said, *"You are not alone."* As that realization set in, I could feel those buried emotions beginning to rise, and for the first time since hearing about Kevin's death, I wept.

When Stephen died, it knocked me down, but I knew that I needed help, so I surrounded myself with friends and family and even sought out grief counselors. And because of that, I was able to get back up on my feet again eventually. But when Kevin died, it knocked me down for good. I didn't seek out friends or family. I didn't talk to counselors or anyone. I lost all motivation to walk down any road of healing. It's not that I didn't want to, it's just that I didn't have the energy to make the journey. Only people that have lost someone close to them will understand how that truly feels. My inner world began to scare me after that. I stopped praying. I stopped worshipping. I even stopped talking to God. And it's not that I was mad at Him, or that I didn't want to do those things, it's just that there was nothing left within me to give. The following days, weeks, and months, I started off each day by using all my strength to say one simple word, "Help." That was my entire prayer life.

There were times, over the next few months, that I would wake up in the morning with a phrase beating in my heart, *"I will be your best friend."* I knew it was God talking to me, but I ignored it on purpose. I wasn't strong enough to have a regular conversation yet, let alone one about friendship. But as much as I tried to ignore it, it would never leave the back of my mind, it just rested there, waiting. And every so often I would see it float its way to the front of my thoughts like a falling feather.

As time went on, I started to grow more nervous that I might fall away from God because I wasn't putting forth any effort into our relationship. I hadn't prayed or worshipped in ages. I felt as if it was only a matter of time before our relationship would sink. But an image would always pop in my head whenever that nervousness would arise, it was of Jesus and me in a rowboat, and He was the only one rowing. I was laid out in the boat, too weak to move. And the boat was always moving forward. I would often think to myself, "Well, I guess we'll really find out if you're the one leading this thing or not." Not having the energy to pray or worship was one of the hardest parts of that season. God was the absolute captain of the ship, or *rowboat*, rather, and that terrified me.

It took about six months for me to open my bible finally. I read one scripture and closed it immediately. It was all I could do. As the days moved on, I began opening it more and more until I was able to read a whole paragraph, and then a chapter. And then one day, I was able to have a conversation with God finally. Apart from waking up and saying, "Help." We hadn't talked in forever. There was a lot of pain and hurt that I had bottled up from not processing it for months. I had seen God weep with me in the depths of my pain when I lost Stephen; I longed for that connection after Kevin died. I just could never bring myself to start the conversation.

The road to healing after Stephen died was *me* choosing God, but the road to healing after Kevin died was *God* choosing me. The Lord would constantly bring me people to ask how I was doing. I didn't pursue anybody. Someone always showed up on the bad days. And even after reconnecting with Jesus again, that phrase never stopped beating in my heart. *"I will be your best friend."* But every time I would hear it, my response was always the same, "I'm not ready to talk about that yet." And He never pushed the issue, I just felt a warm smile in return as the phrase slowly faded away. To be honest, I had already lost two best friends; I didn't want anymore best friends. There was a fear that had taken root in my heart that said: best friends will always leave you. I couldn't handle losing anyone else. And to make sure that happened, I didn't let anyone else in.

I made a lot of mistakes during that time. I closed myself off from a lot of people out of fear of losing them. Even after Louise and I had gotten married the following year, there were times where she had to hold me close and look me in the eyes and say, "Don't shut me out." It was hard. There is no scarier feeling than the fear of losing a loved one. Every time she left the house I thought she was going to die. Every time my parents took a trip, I thought they were going to die. And when that fear crept in, I could feel the urge to pull away from relationships. I had to choose love over fear every day. And I continued to put my faith in a phrase that saved my life once before. "I am not alone. I am not alone. I am not alone." And every time I declared it, I could feel that same beating in my heart, *"I will be your best friend."*

But even though I loved God with all my heart, I was done with having best friends..

... but God was not.

CHAPTER 10

MOVING AT THE SPEED OF WAIT

Something interesting takes place when you surrender your entire heart to God; He often gives it right back, but with a *touch* that brings old things to life. After going through that season with Kevin passing away, I had no choice but to give everything I had to Jesus. I didn't have any strength to keep anything for myself. But in the years that followed, and with the life within me slowly returning, I began to notice the return of something I hadn't felt in a very long time: the desire to create.

One day, a small thought popped into my head. It was very simple -- "I want to create something." Despite its simplicity, its pull was strong. I couldn't get it out of my head. I started thinking about it day and night, and before I knew it, the thought had changed from *I want to create* to *I need to create*. I was suddenly flooded with random ideas that I had never thought of before. I wrote them all down in my phone. I made hundreds of notes! There were stories, observations, revelations, even jokes! I didn't know what to do with them all. It was overwhelming! Little did I know, God was building a foundation within me. A foundation that would reintroduce passions long gone.

After months of writing my thoughts out, I began to discover my voice in creativity. I started sharing my thoughts on social media and with my friends. It blew me away to see that those writings could powerfully impact other people. And as I found my voice, I found something else as well: a forgotten desire for film. I started writing down ideas for stories and even framing shots to go with them. I didn't know why I was doing it. But that small thought had grown much bigger now. *"I need to create. I was born to create."*

I started thinking about film a lot, a whole lot. I even started looking into buying a computer to edit on. I asked God for a confirmation to buy one, but I didn't hear anything back. I prayed for months without hearing an answer. An old thought found its way back into my mind that said maybe this is what I want and not what God wants. And I certainly didn't want to waste thousands of dollars on something that wasn't God-breathed. But as much as I tried, I couldn't get this desire out of my heart. And one day, finally, I heard a soft whisper, *"When you don't hear a response, make a decision off of God's good character."* I asked Louise what she thought. She said she believed in my dreams and would support what I felt. I would have never bought a computer if it wasn't for the support of my wife. So I summoned the courage and said, "I am going to buy a computer out of faith. I don't know if this is God's will, but if it isn't, He will show me because He's good." So Louise and I went out and bought a $2,200 iMac in faith.

I walked out of the Apple store, feeling a bit unsure but excited about the future when we decided to stop by Zales to have Louise's ring cleaned. After handing the ring over to the jeweler, he asked us what brought us to the mall today. I told him that we had just bought a computer for editing. His face lit up as he shouted. "That's awesome! I go to film school in San Francisco." We instantly jumped into a deep conversation about film and different movies. A few minutes later, the ring was ready, but as he went to hand it to us, he looked at me and said, "I have my end of the year thesis coming up, and I still need an editor. Maybe you could edit my film? What do you think?" I was shocked. Literally, five minutes after buying my computer, a door for film had opened up.

In the past, I had tried a thousand times to open doors of opportunity for film, and they were always shut in my face. But this time, it was so easy! I took down his info, and we left. I felt like this was the confirmation that I was looking for. But I was so confused as to why God gave it to me AFTER I had purchased everything and not before. Then I heard His voice, *"You already have what it takes. You just need to believe in yourself first."* Even though I had been getting non-stop ideas for months, I was afraid that maybe God hadn't said anything about it because I still wasn't good enough. And from that time forward, I started getting film job after film job. I never sought out one single opportunity; they always came to me. But every film offer I received, had one thing in common, they were so much bigger than my level of expertise. I always felt in over my head. As much as I wanted to, I couldn't deny the opportunities that God kept bringing me. But the scariest of these opportunities came when a man by the name of Jonathan Welton, offered Louise a job to come work for his online bible school, Welton Academy.

We had met Jonathan while Louise and I were still in our third year of BSSM. I was just about to embark on a water fast, but after realizing that I would probably disappear into thin air from being so skinny, I thought it might be better to change it up. But as I contemplated what to do, I heard the Lord say, *"I want you to go into a time of thanksgiving. Instead of searching out your faults, search out things to be grateful for."* So I did just that. I made a list of everything that I was grateful for, and throughout the day, I would think about that list instead of all the stuff I needed to work on.

A few days into this thanksgiving, I found myself at my church's bookstore. I was browsing through the books when one of them stood out to me. The name of the book was, *School of the Seers*, and for some reason, I was super drawn to it; so I took it home and read it cover to cover. The book was about opening your eyes to see more into the spirit. It really spoke to me and encouraged me through the season I was in. After I finished it, I decided to write down the name of the author on my list of things I was thankful for. The author's name was Jonathan Welton. I began to thank God daily for everything on my list, including this guy, Jonathan. A few days later, I found myself back at church again, but this time, I was walking through the church's coffee shop with Louise. But as we walked, something caught my eye, but this time it wasn't a book, it was a person.

I had to do a double take as I stood in the middle of the busy coffee shop. I saw a man that looked very familiar sitting by himself at a table. I happened to have my new book with me, so I pulled it out to double check, and sure enough, it was the author, Jonathan Welton. I stood there a moment, debating whether or not I should walk up and talk to him. I didn't want to bother him because he was by himself, but then I thought, "You know what? Since I'm going after thanksgiving, I'm going to go up to him and simply thank him for writing the book." So I walked up to him and said, "Excuse me, is your name, Jonathan?" He looked up and smiled, "That's me." He said back. I jumped right into my *thank you*. "I don't mean to bother you; I just wanted to thank you for writing this book. It really ministered to me. That's it. Thanks." I started to walk away, but Jonathan called me back and said, "Hey, wait a second. What's your name?" I told him my name, which led to a few more questions. And before I knew it, he invited Louise and I to come and sit with him to talk for a bit longer. We chatted for about half an hour, and to our surprise, he invited us to have dinner with him the next night, too. And when he left town a few days later, he exchanged numbers with us to keep in contact.

Over the next couple of years, Jonathan would contact us every once in a while to check in on us and see how we were doing. But one day, we got a very different phone call from him. Jonathan called to tell us about an online bible school that he was starting, and how he wanted to offer Louise a job in administration. We prayed about it, but we were already pretty sure it was a massive blessing from heaven.

Louise was perfect for the job, and since the school was all online, she could work from home which was a dream of hers. She took the job and never looked back. I couldn't be happier for her. I honestly thought that Louise would work for Welton Academy and that I would continue home care for people with disabilities, but there was one more unexpected phone call that Jonathan would make, but this time, it was for me.

Jonathan called to say that he was looking to hire a new Welton Academy cameraman, and that he was wondering if I would be interested in the job. My response was, "Um, yeah I would!" I asked him what the job entailed, and he informed me that I would have to travel around to different places, filming all types of various speakers, and then edit and upload the footage every week for students to watch all around the world. I could feel the physical knot in my belly as I tried to keep calm. I had never done anything like that in my entire life. The small film jobs I had been working on paled in comparison. "Um, yeah, I can do those things." I muttered out in response. He asked me how much I charged per hour, a question that I still had no idea how to answer. I was still so new at this; completely out of my league and in over my head. I thought about it for a moment and then suggested a random low number. Jonathan chuckled and then suggested a number four dollars higher. I thought to myself, "This is the strangest interview I've ever been in." But out loud I said, "That's fair. Let's stick with that." And before I knew it, I had become the official School Video Director for Welton Academy.

Years ago, I had tried everything within me to make the prophetic word for film come to pass in my life, but I was always met with resistance. I so desperately wanted to be *the filmmaker* that I got burned out to the point where I didn't care anymore if it happened or not. But there's a big difference between walking through a door that you opened yourself, as opposed to walking through one that God opened for you. If you open it, then it's up to you to keep that door open, but if God opens it, then not even your feelings of *inadequacy* will stop you from walking through it. I had never seen favor like this before. But I also had never been so detached at the same time. I wasn't worried about success anymore. I wasn't concerned with impressing anyone. If God decided to take it all away the next day, I would have been okay with that. The desire for film had been fully surrendered within me, and because of that, film could no longer dictate my significance. If God could still *love* me when I had nothing to offer Him, nothing but the pain and darkness of grieving, then why wouldn't He still love me if I never did film? I accepted Jonathan's offer, not because I felt compelled to fulfill my destiny, but because God asked me to walk through a door that I didn't deserve. I had no idea where this new door would take me, and that's probably a good thing, too, because if I had caught even a glimpse of the different revivalists that I was about to film, I would have run away right there and never looked back.

CHAPTER 11

NEXT STOP, ARGENTINA

For the first time in my life, I couldn't believe I was actually *traveling* for work. Jonathan would fly me to various cities all over America to film different revivalists who would share about their lives. They would preach on evangelism, prophecy, teaching, healing, and so much more. Each speaker had a unique aspect of God that was different from the last. But there was one thing that every trip had in common: I was always so nervous! Meeting all of these generals of the faith was intimidating to say the least. I think sometimes God gets a bit of enjoyment watching us freak out when we're in over our head, mainly because we have to *cling* to Him that much more to survive, so of course, God decided to take things a step further and watch me squirm even more.

As I traveled around the states, the Lord began to give me prophetic words for total strangers that I would eventually meet on whatever trip I was doing at the time. Sometimes they would be a random person at the church, other times it would be for whoever's house I was staying at, but more often than not it was for the speaker themselves! Sometimes those prophetic words would come in a dream, sometimes they would come in a whisper, and sometimes they would randomly pop into my head when I was stuffing my face full of airplane peanuts. But with every new trip, one phrase always stayed on my lips, "Who am I to film these people? Who am I to share these words?" This feeling would be at its highest when I took my first international film trip to Argentina.

Jonathan had received an invitation to Argentina to film all of the Welton Academy curriculum in Spanish. So he and the Welton Academy Mission's Director, Dawn Weaver, took a team of students (and me) to Argentina to minister and film. The day before the trip, I was in my room packing a suitcase, when the Lord started speaking to me about the trip. I suddenly heard a name pop into my head. *"Immanuel."* I stopped packing and wrote down the name in my phone. By this time, I knew to expect a prophetic word before taking a trip. So without even thinking about it, I jotted it down like it was second nature.

As we arrived at the church in Argentina, there was one thing that was very apparent; they had a lot of youth! But the incredible thing is that they were so all so genuinely close to each other. One thing I love about Latin American culture is how family oriented they are. They welcomed us with open arms and open hearts. During the day, we went out into the streets to evangelize with the youth, and at night I would film Welton Academy classes in Spanish. I couldn't believe I was thousands of miles away from my home, getting paid to film in the church and minister in the streets.

One day on the trip, we went on outreach to an impoverished community. Their houses were built with trash, and there was sewage in the streets. My heart broke for them. We went house to house, asking people if they needed prayer. But when we approached the first house, I heard something faint in my spirit, *"Cancer."* And when I set foot in their yard, I had to hold back my shock. Their entire roof was built out of trash. I looked into the eyes of the lady who lived there, and I whispered in my heart, "God. What do you want to say to her?" I immediately heard the name, *"Alejandra."* I asked my interpreter if I could ask a random question. The lady agreed, so I asked her if there was someone close to her named Alejandra. The lady shook her head yes. I then asked if Alejandra was sick. The interpreter asked, and the lady once again shook her head yes. And before I could ask my last question, the lady said through broken English, "Cancer." We gathered in a circle and prayed that Alejandra would be completely healed of cancer.

The very next house a mother and her four daughters came outside to meet us. We prayed and blessed them, but for some reason, the mother seemed very closed off. As I looked at her, I heard the name, *Carlos*, in my heart. I asked her if she knew a man named Carlos. She looked at me and said that it was her brother and that he passed away. I began to pray that all the trauma from his death would be broken off her life. The lady broke down and began to weep. I had to hold back tears of my own as I prayed for her. I knew all too well what it feels like to lose a loved one. Just then, her daughter, who had been silent this whole time, asked if we could pray for her, too. We began to declare that she was pure in God's eyes, and about how much He loved her. She broke down into tears as well. The whole family hugged us tightly as we left.

As hard as my journey had been through losing my best friends, it always felt so good to see the Lord comfort someone in their loss. Feeling God's peace in those moments is like being given a cup of water in the driest desert. Coming into contact with people who had lost someone dear to them would become a regular occurrence in my life after that. Even the very next day, I walked up to a guy in a park and asked him if his name was, Armando. The guy said no, to which at first discouraged me because I had misheard God, but I chose to sit down next to him anyways and have a conversation. He shared with us that he just found out the day before that his mother has cancer. And that his best friend used to take him to church all the time, but that he died the year before. I said I was so sorry, and that I had lost both of my best friends in motorcycle accidents. He looked up at me and said, "That's exactly how my friend died, in a motorcycle accident." I was able to pray that God would help him grieve and that he would find joy once again. His exact response was, "Thank you for making me feel so good because today started off so sad." His face was glowing by the time we left. It was encouraging to see that God could still bless someone just as much, whether or not I got a word of knowledge correct. I guess as long as you *love*, God will always find a way through. And every time my path came across someone who had lost a friend, I would always hear that same beating in my heart. *"I will be your best friend."*

It was strange to go from filming classes one moment to then evangelizing in the streets the next. But as I sat there setting up my camera one night before the service, I began to notice a pattern taking place in my life. I would have thought that with more film opportunities happening for me, it would mean that I would get even fewer chances to do ministry, but that wasn't the case at all. The more I stepped into the world of film; the more my prophetic gifts seem to come alive around me. It's like the two worlds were connected. In the past, I had tried to separate film and my spiritual life into two different sections. One was a *career*, and the other was for *spirituality*. But as I looked at the camera in the midst of that church, I began to wonder if God saw them as the same. Maybe God wanted to encounter me in my film life just as much as my prayer life? - Or maybe He wanted to be included in all sections of my life? -- Or maybe He didn't want my life put into sections at all? --- Or maybe, He wanted it to be just *us*.

Just as the worship was about to begin, a lady came and sat down right next to me. I could tell that she wanted to say something, but for some reason, she wasn't talking. I leaned over to her and said, "Hey, you doing ok?" She looked at me and said, "I know this may sound strange, but I feel like you need to pray for my boyfriend." In my mind, I definitely agreed with her that it felt a bit strange, but on the outside, I said, "Sure, uh, what's his name?" She leaned in a bit closer and said,

"His name is Immanuel. And he's not saved." I instantly remembered back to what the Lord had told me before coming on the trip. I pulled out my phone and showed her the date and time of the note that I had written before coming. She started crying because she knew the Lord was after Immanuel's heart. I prayed for him and over their whole relationship. After that service, I have no idea what happened to them, I never saw her again. But I believe with all certainty, that God is going to encounter Immanuel in a powerful way, and maybe He already has. I mean, it's in his name for crying out loud!

As the worship started, I settled back into my chair and tried to relax a bit. The week had been crazy so far, and everything was happening a mile a minute. It felt good just to have a moment to enjoy God's presence peacefully. But as I sat there, an interesting picture flashed in my mind. It was of a birthday cake with the name, *Daniella,* written on it. The cake was pink, and it had a shiny crown on top. I quickly wrote down the details of the vision in my phone. As I thought about what I had seen, I wondered if I was going to meet a Daniella on outreach later that week. But as often is the case with God, what was about to happen was far greater than I could have imagined.

For the rest of the week, I looked everywhere for a Daniella. We went to hospitals, neighboring churches, out on the streets, but it was no use. I couldn't find a single person with that name. I had begun to think that maybe it had been just my imagination and not God at all. But on the last night of the trip, out team stopped to minister at an orphanage in town. I had arrived late because I had been filming all afternoon, so when I got there, the team was about to pray for the kids. I walked in and saw boys and girls everywhere, ranging from all sorts of ages. I looked around and noticed a young girl sitting nearby, so I walked up and asked if I could join them in prayer. As I sat down, one of the team members asked the young girl what her name was. The young girl replied, *"Nu Rita."* One of the team members began to prophesy that they saw a crown being placed on her head. When she said the word, crown, I instantly thought of the vision I had earlier that week. As I looked at Nu Rita, I began to feel that the word was somehow for her. It confused me because I knew her name wasn't Daniella, but somehow I just knew it.

When it was my turn to pray, I waited a moment for God to interpret what that vision meant for Nu Rita. And as I looked into her eyes, I heard the Lord say what it meant. I shared that I also felt she would be getting a crown and even though she was older now, God was making it a pink crown; due to the pain of her childhood. I could see tears beginning to form in her eyes. I started to share about how her birthday hasn't always been a good day in the past, but that God was going to redeem it. And that her next birthday was going to be a great one. At this point, I was confident the word was for her. But I was still confused as to why the birthday cake said the name, *Daniella*, on it. I asked her if she knew anyone by the name of Daniella, to which she replied no. I sat there for a moment, completely stumped, I began to feel a bit of discouragement come back as if I had maybe gotten it wrong. But just as I was about to move on, a small thought popped into my head. I looked at her and said, "During a church service this week, I saw a picture of a birthday cake with the name Daniella on it as well as a pink crown. I thought I was going to meet a Daniella. But now what I feel like I'm supposed to do is to describe to you who my sister is, whose name is *Daniella*. And everything I describe will be who God says you are. Is that ok with you?" She smiled and nodded her head yes.

I said to her, "Nu Rita, my sister Daniella is a very strong woman. She is one of the most loving people I've ever met. She protects the people she loves and would give them the shirt off her back if she had to. She will always go to bat for me, and if anyone messes with me, they will have to deal with her. She can also be stubborn, in a good way *(Nu Rita laughed)*. But that's because she cares so much about the people around her. She is one of the strongest people I've ever seen." And then I said with a laugh, "Come to think of it; you actually look like my sister a bit."

The translator then asked Nu Rita what she was feeling. She pointed at me and began to speak in Spanish. Through the translator, she told us that everything I had just described about my sister fit her perfectly and that it was funny that I described a birthday cake because her birthday was just last week. But not just any birthday, it was her 15th birthday. In Latin American culture, a young girl's 15th birthday is called a quinceanera. It's pretty much the biggest day of her life besides her wedding. Her friends wanted to throw her a party, but she told them to cancel it because she was too sad. Nu Rita went on to say that she felt known that God would want to redeem her birthday. I pulled out my phone to show her what I had written so she could see it with her own eyes, but as I read the note to her, I noticed the date it was written; *May 8th.* I realized that it had been almost a week. I looked at her and said, "Nu Rita, I wrote this on May 8th. When was your birthday?" She put her hand to her mouth and gasped. Her birthday was on May 8th. I put my hand on her shoulder and said, "Nu Rita, on your 15th birthday, your quinceanera, God spoke to me about you. He knows you. He loves you. And wants to change your life." As the tears grew in her eyes, she couldn't decide whether to laugh or cry. I gave her a big hug; she didn't let me go for a long time. She held on so tightly and just kept saying, "Thank you. Thank you."

I could write pages and pages of what God did on that trip alone. Everything from seeing the youth of the church getting so impacted that they stayed up till 6 AM prophesying over each other. To supernaturally understanding a lady on the streets who only spoke Spanish; I still don't know how that happened, but it did. To randomly getting invited to film Carlos Annacondia himself; a revivalist that so profoundly affected the country, that Christians there use the phrase,

"Before and after Annacondia," when referring to the church in Argentina. Oh, and of course, when I first met Carlos, the Lord started speaking to me about a *Rebecca* in his life. I didn't want to share it with him out of fear of getting it wrong, and the fact that this man changed the landscape of Argentina. It was the ultimate, "Who am I to say this, God!?" But I eventually got over myself and took the risk anyway. And to my surprise, the name Rebecca certainly meant something to him. It was his daughter. It finally dawned on me that these big name people were just regular people like you and I. They went through hardships and bad days just like the rest of us. But so often, people don't encourage them because they're too afraid. I apologized to God that day for always being difficult when asked to give words to high-level leaders. I could feel God's passion for comforting them. How could I deny Him that? As much as it scared me, I told the Lord that I would give those words to leaders whenever He wanted me to. Sometimes when you are making deals with God, you have absolutely no idea what you're signing up for; this is one of those moments. Because when I returned home to America, God was about to take these *words of knowledge* to a whole new level.

CHAPTER 12

A DREAM COME TRUE

When I got home from Argentina, my travel began to ramp up even more. At one point, I was flying every weekend and sometimes two times a week. Every time we crossed a name off the list of speakers, it felt like two more were added in its place. But as I looked over the upcoming speakers, one particular name caught my eye. It was a man by the name of James Goll. James was a seer prophet that lived out of Nashville, Tennessee. I had never met him before, but that wasn't why it caught my eye; I had a dream about James three years before that.

In the dream, I was standing on a street directly in front of a house that I had never seen before. But as I stood there, a man came jogging towards me as he went for a run on the street. When he got closer, I noticed that it was actually James Goll and that the house I was standing in front of was his. His home had a sort of East coast look, and there were steps with a railing that went up to the door. I began to talk to him as he walked up the steps, but right in the middle of our conversation, I instantly woke up. I thought the dream was bizarre because I had no connection to James whatsoever. But as I told Louise about the dream, I decided to write it down in my phone anyway. The day I had the dream was on March 17, 2014. Which just so happened to be Saint Patrick's Day. At the time, I wasn't even working for Welton Academy or doing film at all.

Three years later...

As I stood there looking at the list, I leaned over to Louise and said, "Oh my gosh, do you remember that dream I had where I went to James Goll's house?" Now let me explain to you, on most of these trips I film the speakers in their home church, their personal office, a rented building, etc. But this time was different. She looked closely at the list and then back at me to say. "It says that he's personally requested that you film at his house." I sat there in silence as the details of the dream came flooding back. The steps, the running, the railing, even the look of the house. I couldn't help but smile. I knew that another God adventure was awaiting me.

I could feel knots in my stomach when the day finally came to film in Nashville. It's not that I was afraid, I was just bursting with anticipation. I woke up at the hotel and got ready to head over to his house. But as I drove there, I couldn't help but think of the different details of the dream. Since landing in Nashville, I hadn't seen any houses at all that looked like the one in my dream. The house in my dream was very particular; it had big stairs with long railings. And because of that, I was almost certain that his home wouldn't look like it did in my dream. I thought maybe the details that I saw were going to be more *symbolic* than *literal*. But that thought would change when I drove into his housing community. Suddenly, I found myself in a neighborhood where the look of the houses all began to change dramatically. To be honest, the closer I got, the more nervous I became. That's when I heard the GPS on my phone say, "You've reached your destination." I looked to my left, and there it was. The *exact* same house, the same stairs, the same railing, the same everything from my dream.

I began to slowly pull my film equipment from the car as I stood in the driveway, but at the same time, I couldn't peel my eyes from the house. The longer I stood there, the more nervous I became, and to be honest, as I unloaded my equipment, I was slightly trembling. I walked up the stairs and knocked on the door. Through the window, I could see James slowly approaching. As I stood there waiting, I couldn't help but stare at the intricate details of the stairs and railing. *"I saw this in my dream."* I thought quietly to myself. Suddenly, the door opened, and I looked up to see a man standing before me with a huge smile on his face. "Lopez?" He asked. "That's me!" I said with a laugh as I began to carry my gear inside. One thing I noticed right away was how relational and down to earth he was. It made me feel a lot more relaxed, which was very helpful because in the back of my mind a small part of me was screaming. *"What is happening!? I've seen this place in my dreams! I've been here before!! What does this mean?!"* So that was a plus.

In the past, whenever I suspected there was a *God encounter* waiting for me, I always found it so hard to relax at the moment. I think it was because I didn't want to miss it. So I would always pray super hard leading up to the moment. But it sometimes left me with hope deferred because I would put different expectations on it that were never meant to be put there in the first place. Nowadays, whenever I suspect God is about to do something, I merely say, "Thank you God that you will make this happen in my life. I won't miss it. I'll hear your voice. I'll see the sign. Whatever it is, I won't miss it because you're good." Changing that mindset took the pressure off of me, and I was finally able to enjoy those moments as God intended.

Over the next hour or so, we got to know each other while I set up the equipment. I talked about where I was from and how I came to live in Redding. He shared about his family and how he had just recently gotten back surgery. But as we talked, I was listening quietly at the same time for God's voice moving forward. When you no longer feel pressure to make a moment happen, you can rest in knowing that He'll speak to you when He wants you to move. As the conversation continued, somehow we came upon the topic of dreams. There was a small break in the conversation, and I felt the moment hit, *"Share it."* I heard. I didn't hesitate. "This may sound weird, but I had an interesting dream before I came here." James' ears instantly perked up. "Oh really?" He said. "Tell me about it." I began to share that three years ago on Saint Patrick's Day, I had a dream that I came to his house. And that his house looked exactly like it did in the dream. I went on to say, "I saw you going for a run on the street." He instantly stopped me. "You said I was running?" He asked. "Yeah, you were going for a jog," I replied. He smiled and said, "You don't know what that means. Right before you arrived, I was reading a note from my doctor concerning my back. Mind you; I haven't been able to run in years. But he told me to start taking light walks around my neighborhood. Then eventually, I can move up to jogging. And how it will eventually help me to run." He perked up even more in his seat. "Okay, let's break down this dream."

I didn't know that James had written a book on dream interpretation and how much knowledge he had on it. We began to break down the dream piece by piece and what it meant. Every step of the way, he continually asked me questions to see if I could find the answers on my own. I could tell he was definitely a teacher at heart. Each detail that we broke down spurred on different stories and incredible experiences about the prophetic. He then asked me, "Who was the dream centered around?" I thought about it for a moment. "I felt like the dream was centered around you." I replied. "And what were you doing in the dream?" He continued. "I was observing you," I answered back. "And what are we doing today?" He asked with a smile. I said, "I'm filming you. So I'm observing you again at your house." It was crazy the number of details and layers he broke down from the dream. Way more than I ever saw or could ever have known on my own. And what made it even crazier is that when I first had that dream in March 2014, he wasn't even living in that house yet, he was living somewhere else, but then in June 2014, he moved into the house that I saw in my dream. There were so many layers.

He went on to share that the house we were in was actually his dream home. His realtor had given him a list of houses to choose from, and without even viewing the house, he put an offer on the one God told him to buy. I stopped him mid-sentence, "Wait a second. You mean to say you didn't even look at the house before buying it?" He laughed and replied, "Nope." I was shocked. He then pointed at a room to my left and said, "I've always wanted a house with an upper room and a recording studio." I looked over to see a closed room with platinum records hanging by the door. "What are those?" I asked curiously. He smiled, and then said back, "*I Can Only Imagine* was recorded in that studio." My mouth dropped open. I couldn't believe it. But before I could even respond, James whipped around and shouted, "And that's why you're here! God is going to take you into the upper room of media and show you things that you can only imagine!" Anytime I've ever shared the story of meeting James Goll; I have only ever shared that *last part* with my wife. Needless to say, I was completely wrecked in that moment.

After filming him, he walked over to his bookcase and said, "So, which of my books do you have?" He grabbed a stack of them and started handing them to me, "Here, you can have these. You'll like that dream interpretation one." He said with a laugh. As I packed my gear into the car, I couldn't help but look back at the house and then to my new stack of books sitting next to me. I don't think I'll ever get used to God adventures. I had many different ups and downs over the previous three years, victories and defeats, but God still managed to get me to exactly where I needed to be. For some reason, that realization deeply encouraged me. No matter the cards you give God, He can always find a winning hand.

CHAPTER 13

THE BUSH BUSH

In addition to working for Welton Academy, I often got film offers to do other jobs on the side as well. But one, in particular, would take me to a place that I never thought I would set foot. It all started one day at Bethel; I happened to run into Shara Pradhan, the woman who had prophesied me moving to Redding in the first place to do BSSM. I thanked her for speaking into my life all those years ago. But as we talked, I was surprised to find out that she was actually pursuing a career in film as well. We stayed in contact after that, and as we got to know each other over the following months, she would eventually ask me to edit her first short film. Shara and I worked really well together, we seemed to speak the same language in creativity, and as time went on, she became like a big sister to me. Anytime I was living below the standard that God set for my life; she would always call me out and push me higher. I owe her so much. Shara would later get married to the amazing Danny Chalmers and become Shara Chalmers. One of my greatest honours in life was being asked to be a groomsman at their wedding. One day, I got a phone call from Shara saying that she had been asked to work on a documentary, but that she wouldn't sign on if I couldn't work with her, too. It was *classic* Shara; always fighting for me. And the next thing I know, I was on a plane to Mozambique, Africa, where we would be following someone who had been there the first night I met Shara all those years ago -- a lady by the name of Heidi Baker.

It took us 48 hours of straight travel and three continents to get from Redding, California to Pemba, Mozambique. I can't describe how run down and fatigued my body felt when we finally arrived at Heidi's ministry base there. Traveling across the world is one thing, but traveling across the world while transporting a ton of film equipment is another thing entirely. When we made it through the airport in Pemba, we were greeted by a sea of kids who had been eagerly awaiting our arrival. It became an endless wave of hugs and greetings, but with a nine-hour time difference starting to set in, I could feel the faces in front of me becoming a slow blur.

Even though the base and the airport were only a few minutes apart, the drive that separated them was eye-opening in itself. On the streets, you would see guards carrying assault rifles across their chest, mothers carrying baskets on top of their heads, and children carrying slightly smaller children on their tiny hips. For a few brief moments, I had completely forgotten just how tired I was as I stared out the window. And just like clockwork, a Mozambican voice came from the backseat of the car and said, "Welcome to Africa."

When we arrived at the base, I was shocked to see just how big it was. There were kids and youth everywhere. As we pulled up to the front gate, there was a soccer game of about 30 kids playing in the dirt. I got excited about playing soccer with them, but at the moment, even the thought of getting out of the car made me feel tired. After driving towards the middle of the base, we eventually stopped at the guest housing. We got out of the car and began to lug our gear through the dirt as we were shown to our room. I opened the door to see six wooden bunk beds with large mosquito nets draped over them. I had to take a deep breath as I began to unpack my gear. I had never done anything like this before in my entire life. I don't even like camping, and here I was in the midst of Mozambique, Africa, with tattered safety nets to keep out the malaria-filled mosquitoes. I could feel God trying to hold back His laughter.

By the time we finally finished unloading our film equipment, it was starting to get dark outside. But because it was barely evening time, we still had to fight to stay awake or else we would never get adjusted to the new time zone. I had overheard that there was a church service that had just started on the base, so I brought myself to attend to help fight the sleepiness. As I stood there in worship, like a zombie, a small boy approached me and stuck his hand out to shake mine. He was maybe seven or eight; his bright white smile pierced through a dirt covered face. I stuck out my hand to shake his, but he switched his hand around and moved his thumb on top of mine, and before I knew it, we were in an all-out thumb war. I purposely began to cheat with my pinky just to make him laugh; his smile managed to grow even bigger. From his other hand, he revealed a cracker that seemed to be covered with some sort of cream. He offered it to me, but I said I wasn't very hungry. He then looked down at my water and asked for a drink. I smiled and nodded yes, so he reached down and took in about five huge gulps before wiping his mouth with an expressive, *"Ahhhhhhh."*

After drinking the rest of the water, he set the bottle down and put his arm around my waist. I was surprised at how friendly he was without even knowing me. I bent down and asked him what his name was. He had to speak over the loud worship music, so he grabbed my head and pulled it close. He said a Mozambican name that I didn't understand, but I nodded and told him my name, too. He nodded back, letting go of my head and immediately returning his arm to my waist as he watched the band play. I stood up straight, and after a moment, I placed my arm around his tiny shoulder and held him close. I laughed to myself at how precious this little boy was, but after a few minutes of standing there, something amazing started to happen.

As we stood there, arm in arm, both watching the band on stage, I began to feel God's presence begin to cover my back and shoulders and then my head like a thick warm blanket. I don't know why, but it startled me at first. Maybe it's because I was so tired from the travel or perhaps it's because my mind had been too much in *film mode*. But as I closed my eyes, I found myself having to fight back tears. It's hard to describe how refreshing that was. It was like being able to breathe again. I raised my other arm and began to worship and sing along with the band. My body may have wanted to sleep, but I think my spirit needed this even more. I half expected the boy to leave after a few minutes, but to my surprise, he stayed there with his tiny arm firmly around my waist and worshipped right along with me. It was in that moment; a thought slowly began to drift into my mind. *"I think this trip could have more in store for me than I thought."*

In Mozambique, when you go on outreach to surrounding villages, they call it going into the *bush*, but when you go DEEP into the bush, they call it going into *the bush bush*. Every outreach we did that week was into the bush bush. And there wasn't one single day that we didn't get stopped by Mozambican police, and the first time they didn't let us leave until we gave them a thousand mets. Which at first I was like, "Oh my gosh, we just gave them a thousand dollars!" But then I looked at the exchange rate; it was like 15 bucks and change. The first outreach we went on; we drove hours into the bush bush to a remote village that had never heard the name of Jesus before. On the way, we accidentally hit a chicken on the road, and it got stuck in the grill of the van. As we arrived at the village, they ripped the dead chicken out of the grill and cooked it for us to eat. That was -- um, *new*. Later that night, they held a meeting for the surrounding tribes to come and attend. We saw blind eyes open, deaf ears healed, all caught on film. So many people gave their lives to Jesus that night. The next morning, Heidi personally poured coffee for everyone that was present; tribe leaders, grandmothers, children, our team, everyone. She took the time to speak to each one individually.

Following Heidi around that week was unlike anything I had ever seen before. Everywhere we went, she would stop and take the time to minister to whoever was in front of her. It was like no one else in the world at that moment mattered but that person. Before that trip, I had no idea that Heidi had transformed the entire landscape of Mozambique, and that the government often came to her for help. It was incredible to see that someone could love a nation back to Jesus one single person at a time. When I look back, I can't help but feel like I was standing in the midst of a modern day Mother Theresa. One time, when I was sitting in the front seat, desperately trying to get a steady camera shot as we drove through an off-road shortcut, Heidi leaned over to me and asked me where I was from. I was a bit taken aback by her question at first. I set my camera down and told her I lived in Redding, California. Her immediate response was, "Oh, do you go to Bethel?" I laughed and said that I did. She then went on to say that she had a home there and loves to visit whenever she can. There are moments in your life, where it feels like you step outside yourself for just a moment, and you watch what's happening around you. This was one of those moments. As we talked, I thought to myself, "Am I really traveling through the Mozambican outback in a Jeep with Heidi Baker, chatting about my life?" It was weird to think how the avenue of film had opened up so many doors that I could have never opened on my own. Favor is strange because it constantly puts you places that you don't always feel worthy to be a part of. I think God loves to remind us that the only reason we are where we are, is because of one thing and one thing only: *underserved grace*.

When we arrived at the village, Heidi shared with us that they had been drilling unsuccessfully for over two years to find water. The villagers were forced to walk an entire day just to get water, but just as we pulled up, something incredible happened. I got out of the car and turned on my camera, but as soon as I looked over at the working drill, a geyser of water came spurting up from the ground beneath it. I looked over at Heidi and saw that she was jumping up and down with joy. Crowds of people started flooding in to drink the fresh water. They brought cups, buckets, anything they could get their hands on. As they began to drink from the endless stream of water that was shooting from the earth, it didn't take long before they started playing around in it. Everyone from the oldest grandma to the tiniest kid was playing in the water that day. They were splashing each other with smiles so big on their faces that I will never forget them. I couldn't help myself, I set down my camera and ran into the spraying fountain of water to join in the excitement. Everyone was hugging each other with such joy and happiness. As I watched the faces of the villagers around me, I felt like I was starting to see a part of God's heart that I had never seen before.

Every time we went on outreach, Heidi would show a movie to the villagers called *The Jesus Film*. They would set up a tiny projector and an enormous white screen in the middle of the bush bush, as crowds of people from miles around would come to see what was taking place. I sat there observing, as hundreds upon hundreds of people heard the name of Jesus for the first time. It was a form of the gospel that not many are used to in America. I'll be honest with you; if any small part of me considered sharing the gospel a task, I got to see it for what it really is; a complete honour.

Their faces were glued to the screen, and their eyes didn't blink. Hundreds of them; men, women, and children sat quietly in the middle of nowhere out in the African bush. I would scan the crowd slowly just to watch their reactions, only to find myself pausing on random people's expressions as I wondered what they thought. My eyes drifted upwards, and every star in the sky seemed so close that you could touch it, with no electricity for miles, the clarity was piercing. But as I stared into the night, something else caught my eye.

During the middle of the film, Heidi walked over to the front and sat down with the kids. As she was getting comfortable, she squeezed a few of them, but then turned her attention towards the bright screen. I thought to myself how she must have seen this film over a thousand times. When you do outreach every week for 21 years, you have to be sick of this cheesy 1979 film by now. But as I sat there watching, her face told a different story.

A few moments later, her eyes seemed to light up in amazement; her mouth held slightly open as if watching it for the first time. Even as the scenes changed, so did her expressions. I thought to myself, " How could she still be so interested in this film after 21 years." But as I sat there watching, suddenly, the screen went dark, and I couldn't see anything. They had just rolled the rock over Jesus' tomb in the movie. A few moments later, the projector lit up again as the scene changed. But as I looked back towards Heidi, I noticed something else had changed as well. Her eyes were now shut, and she was praying quietly under her breath.

That's when it hit me. Heidi can sit through the same old movie, week after week, not because she puts up with it, but because it reminds her of her best friend. She can travel aimlessly out into the bush for hours on end, not because she feels like she has to, but because she feels absolutely compelled to. And she can lay in the dirt for 21 years, not because she feels the need to earn God's love, but because that's where she *sees* Jesus the most. As I sat there watching her, I couldn't help but think to myself, "I want to know you like that, Jesus. I want to be that close to you." And before I could even realize what I was saying, I could feel that familiar phrase beating deep within my heart. *"I will be your best friend."* The reality is that I secretly longed to have that friendship in my heart, but I didn't want to say it out loud because that would be admitting to it. I was still terrified to allow anyone into that place, even God -- *especially* God. But as I sat there in the night, watching Heidi sit with her best friend, I wondered if my life would ever come to that place as well.

CHAPTER 14

HEART'S DESIRE

As I returned home to America, I often thought of that night with Heidi in Mozambique. There was a part of me, deep down, that began to imagine a life where God and I could be best friends. But I would never admit that to myself. And every time I thought about it, I could feel an anxiety begin to rise up within me. There was a lot of buried pain and fear that I didn't want to face. I was still afraid that if I let the Lord into that place, He would just let me down. I knew God was *good*, I knew He was *trustworthy*, but as anyone with trauma can tell you, pain doesn't always make sense logically. I wished I could trust Him that way; it just didn't seem possible anymore. But little did I know, God would go to great lengths to gently mend the fabric of that trust, thread by thread.

I want to stop right here and explain something that you may not know about me. I am a huge dog lover. If there was ever a statement that couldn't be stressed enough in this entire world, it's that one. If I had to be somewhere in five minutes, and I happened to see a dog along the way, I would gladly stop to pet it. If I saw a dog in a car by himself, I wouldn't think twice about standing awkwardly near the window just to say hi. They are undoubtedly the best animal there ever was. And that's not an opinion, that's a fact. I'm sure someone somewhere has done a study because dogs are amazing.

I had wanted a dog for years, but it just didn't seem possible with all the travel I was doing. I would always get sad looking at photos of dogs on the internet. And to be honest, I was even following quite a few dogs on social media. But what made it even sadder, is that they always had way more followers than I did. They had like thousands and thousands of people following them, which I guess makes sense, because they're dogs, and dogs are amazing. But as time went on, I longed to have a dog of my own more and more.

One day, I heard a testimony of a married couple that had just gotten a dog. But the funny thing is, the wife absolutely hated dogs, while the husband loved them. The husband kept asking his wife if they could get a dog, but she always said no. He kept on persisting over and over again until she finally gave in and said, "Fine! If you can find a dog that meets all of these requirements, then we can bring it home." She handed him a long, detailed list that was insanely specific. She knew there would be no way that he could find a dog that met her list of random details. But that was all the husband needed, he took the list and started asking God to bring them that exact dog. And wouldn't you know it, someone contacted them shortly after, asking if they knew of a home that would be willing to take in a dog. This particular dog met every single detail on the list, and so the husband was able to bring the dog home to his happy wife.

I really love that testimony. Shortly after hearing it, I decided to write out my own list of a dog that I wanted. I knew it wasn't possible to have a dog because of our travel schedule; I was more so curious to see what came out on the list. This was my list: Boston Terrier, male, stronger build, loves to play, lots of energy, no bug eyes, and fully trained. As I looked over the list, it seemed like the best dog there ever was. And without even realizing it, I found myself saying to God, "I don't know how you would do it, but would you be able to bring me this dog?" It seemed like such an impossible request. But I just kept thinking to myself, "If you could do it for that husband, then you can do it for me." And just like so many times before, I had a dream.

A few months later after writing the list, I had a dream that my mom had bought a Boston Terrier. In the dream, the dog ran up and jumped up on me so hard that it almost knocked me over. I held him in my arms while he licked my face. I suddenly woke up from the dream to a room with no dog anywhere in sight. It made me sad to think about how impossible all that was. My mom hadn't ever mentioned wanting to get a dog, and I don't even think she knew what a *Boston Terrier* was. But I knew for a fact that my dad did NOT want a dog. The dogs we had when we were younger caused a lot of damage to our house, so my dad didn't want a dog ever again. I told Louise about the dream and how it made me sad that it would never happen. But just three days after that dream, I got an interesting phone call.

I was out and about in Redding when my phone started to ring. I checked to see who it was and saw that it was my mom. I picked up but it seemed like she was already halfway through a sentence when she started talking, "You need to come to our house right now. I saw a lady post online about how she was selling a dog, and without even thinking about it, I told her that I was interested and for her to bring the dog over. But you have to come here now because I barely got your father to agree just to see the dog. I need some help convincing him." My exact response back to her was, "WHAT?! You want to buy a dog? What kind of dog is it?" She paused for a second as if trying to remember what the post had said, "Um, it's like a Boston Terrier or something." I started freaking out as I screamed, "OH MY GOSH! I just had a dream a few nights ago that you bought a Boston Terrier!" My mom shouted back, "What?! Are you serious? You need to get over here right now. The lady is on her way! Come. Here. Now!" I hung up the phone and raced to my parent's house. As I drove there, I could still picture the dog in my mind from my dream. I kept saying out loud, "If that dog is the same one from my dream, I will know it."

Next thing I know, I am sitting on my parent's couch, and there is a lady knocking on the front door. I could feel the sweat on my hands as my mom got up to let her in. When she opened the door, I was speechless. The dog she held in her hands was the EXACT same dog from my dream. She sat down on the other end of the couch and began to ask us questions. I tried my best to look calm on the outside, but on the inside, I was freaking out. We chatted for a few minutes, and it was all going nice and well until my mom decided to change the topic suddenly. After a brief pause in the conversation, my mom looked at me and said, "Sweetie, tell her about the dream you had the other night." Instantly, I could feel all the blood in my body rush directly to my face. My eyes widened as I slowly turned my gaze back towards my mom. I tried to send a subtle hint that I was not about to look like a crazy person in front of this lady. "Um, what, what are you -- what are you talking about?" I asked with a forced laugh. My mom did not get the hint. She kept talking, "The dream that you told me about. You know the one with the Boston Terrier and stuff." It was a *classic* mom move. There was no going back now. I turned back towards the lady holding the dog and tried to play it off, "Oh, yeah, um, that's right, I did have a dream, yeah. Well, I had a dream three nights ago that my mom had bought a Boston Terrier, and, well, I think it was that exact Boston Terrier." The following moments of silence were the longest and the most awkward of any in my entire life. I remember thinking to myself, "Yup, this lady thinks I'm crazy."

I didn't want to be the first one to speak after that, well, to be honest, it was more so that I just didn't know what else to say. I had no clue what this lady's beliefs were. So I just sat there, staring, waiting for something to happen. But then out of absolutely nowhere, the lady suddenly burst into tears and said, "I just want him to go to a nice home. I just want him to be with a nice family. And I really feel like that family is you." I was stunned. I had no idea what made her say that, and frankly, I didn't want to ask. I just smiled and said, "He is going to be so loved here. I promise." We gave the lady a big hug as she took some time to say goodbye to the dog, and before I knew it, she was gone. And I was left staring face to face with a Boston Terrier named Oscar. My dad still wasn't all too happy about getting a dog. He just kept saying over and over again, "He's on probation. If he does even one thing wrong, ONE, he's outta here!" I didn't need any convincing at all that this dog was heaven sent. He met everything on my list. Every, single, thing. But if that wasn't enough, God was about to do something that not even my father could deny.

A few days after getting Oscar, I had heard about a private meeting in town with a guy named Shawn Bolz. To say that Shawn is prophetic is quite an understatement. It's not uncommon for Shawn to start calling out people's names, addresses, illnesses, etc. while he's preaching. I really, really wanted to get a prophetic word from the Lord in that meeting. So the night before, I stayed up all night long praying that I would get one. I'm sure no one else has done that, right? I even texted some prophetic friends saying, "Going to a Shawn Bolz meeting tomorrow, pray I get a word!" Even as Louise and I drove to the meeting the next day, I kept declaring out loud, "I'm gonna get a word from Shawn! I'm gonna get a word from Shawn!" I was surprised to see how many people could fit into a small house where the meeting was held. People were standing, sitting, leaning against walls, whatever they had to do to get inside. Shawn began sharing his heart for a bit and then went into some prophetic time. My first thought was, "This is it. I'm gonna get a prophetic word." He went around the room, calling out people that God was highlighting to him. After a while, he paused for a moment and then said, "Was someone here born on August, 13th 1989?" My hand shot up in the air as fast as it could. I wasn't born on that day, but *Louise* was. I wanted to make sure we claimed it before anyone else could say anything.

Shawn looked at Louise for a second, and then went on to say, "I am hearing the Lord say that He is going to bring redemption back to the *Watkins* family." Watkins was Louise's maiden name. He started prophesying about her family history and all that God was going to do, and then he asked, "Who are *Juan* and *Irene.*" With tears in her eyes, Louise replied, "Those are my in-laws." Shawn then began sharing what he felt the Lord was going to do in their lives over the next two years." *(Which all came to pass by the way).* Then Shawn paused for a moment, as if not sure how to explain the next part. I sat up in my seat, waiting for my word now. Then Shawn continued, "This is gonna sound strange, but I have a Boston Terrier at home, and for some reason…" But before Shawn could even finish, Louise jumped in, "We just got a Boston Terrier!" Shawn laughed to himself, and then finally said, "God is going to use this dog to bring healing to your family." I laughed at the fact that Louise got a word, then Louise's family, then my parents, and then my dog! Everybody in my family got a word! But now, it was my turn. I sat up even more in my seat as I prepared myself for destiny. Shawn then looked right at me, paused for a slight moment, and then decided to move on to someone else. *Ouch.*

As happy as I was for everyone else, it stung a little that I didn't get a word, too. I couldn't believe it. I mean, I was the one who stayed up all night long praying. I was the one who had been making declarations all day. And what happened? Everyone got a word but me, even my dog got a word before I did! It was so ridiculous that I had to just laugh it off and let it go. And that word from Shawn Bolz all but sealed my dad's fate in his losing argument after that. But to be honest, it didn't take long for my mom and I to catch my dad saying to Oscar, "Who's a good boy? Who's a good boy?!" And even with my crazy travel schedule, I was still able to have a dog that lived at my parent's house. It was perfect. This dog was truly heaven sent. And as time went on, not getting a prophetic word turned into a funny story about how my *dog* is more blessed than I am. But as often is the case with God, what we see in front of us isn't always the final chapter.

CHAPTER 15

ECLIPSED BY GOODNESS

After seeing God bring me the dog of my dreams *(literally)*, I started to wonder what other desires of my heart He was interested in. There were certain parts of who God was that I had seen many times before; things like strength, healing, deliverance, prophecy. But when he brought me, Oscar, I started to understand just how much He cares about the *little* things in life. It was like a kindness I had never seen before. And as my film journey continued, I kept that in the back of my mind.

So many of my experiences with God seem to take me back to Nashville, Tennessee; maybe because that's where it all started, I don't know. But this time would prove to be different than the others. I was nearby Nashville in Florence, Alabama, filming a speaker that I came to meet when they informed me that there was going to be a Solar Eclipse the following day. I had heard about an upcoming Eclipse happening, but I had read that it wasn't going to be viewable from where I lived in California. He went on to tell me that it was going to be very clear from that section of America. I started to get excited about the possibility of viewing a full Solar Eclipse. I asked him when the exact time of the eclipse would be, and to my surprise, it was going to take place during my flight back home. I couldn't believe I was about to see a Solar Eclipse from 39,000 feet in the air.

I thought it would be no problem at all just to pick up some Eclipse glasses before leaving town, at least that's what I had hoped. But after going from place to place, to place, to more places -- I was quickly informed that the entire city had been sold out for weeks. I even followed up on a tip about a guy selling them out of his trunk in the Hobby Lobby parking lot. But all I found there was another man also looking for the *Hobby Lobby Guy*. We were both sad when the Hobby Lobby Guy informed us that he was indeed sold out as well.

I sat quietly in my car in the middle of the parking lot, feeling a bit sad. I was going to be on a flight the very next day, during a full-on Solar Eclipse, but with no way to see it! I couldn't think of any more places to visit or call. I was completely out of ideas; when one last thought suddenly popped into my head. *'Why don't I just ask God to bring me one?'* I had tried everything else, what did I have to lose? So I closed my eyes and said, "God, where are some Eclipse glasses? I need a pair." I immediately heard the phrase, *"Newton Street."* I grabbed my phone and typed in Newton Street into the GPS to see if it even existed; and not only did it exist, it was only four minutes away. I literally screamed out loud, "Let's go on an adventure, God!" I put my car in drive and drove off.

A few minutes later, I arrived at Newton Street. It was a residential neighborhood which honestly confused me. My heart was beating, and I was nervous, but I was more excited than anything. I thought to myself, "Am I just gonna knock on a door or something? Not sure what to do here exactly, God." But before I could even finish that thought, a man standing in front of his house started waving at me as I drove by. As I looked over at him, I noticed that he started to walk towards my car. At this point, he was making hand motions for me to stop. So I slowed the car and rolled down my window and said, "How are you doing? You wouldn't happen to have an extra pair of those Eclipse glasses would you?" He smiled and said back in a soft voice,

"No sir, don't even have a pair of those for myself." *"Oh,"* I said out loud, wondering why he waved me down in the first place. Immediately, the guy points at my radio and says, "You listening to gospel?" I looked over to see worship playing softly on the radio. "Oh. Yeah, I am actually." The man just looked at me and smiled. I smiled back. "Are you a Christian?" I asked. His smile got even bigger, "Yes, I am." he answered. I started to realize that I probably wasn't going to get any Eclipse glasses on Newton Street. But I still had no idea what I was doing there.

I took a step of faith and said, "This may sound kinda crazy, but I was just out and about looking for Eclipse glasses, and I couldn't find any at all, so I asked God where to go and I felt led to come here." His face changed like he was a bit shocked. I continued further, "Do you need prayer for anything in particular? Anything at all." He looked up and off into the distance, took a deep breath and then looked back at me, "Can't say that I do, to be honest." He replied. I sat there for a moment, not sure what to do exactly. There was a mini conversation/ freak out with God in my head going on, *"Why am I here? This guy doesn't have glasses. He doesn't need prayer. Why am I here?"* I took a moment and then looked back over to him and said, "Well, maybe God just wants you to know that He was thinking of you. He loves you very much. And He brought me all the way over here just to say *that* to you." His face filled with a warm smile again. "Thank you very much." He said softly. We made small talk for a bit before I finally took off. I drove away so curious as to what just happened. I still had a 2-hour drive ahead of me to Nashville, so I decided to leave town and head that way. I looked up to God and said, "Alright, you're just gonna have to give me a pair of glasses tonight in Nashville because I'm running out of time."

That 2-hour drive was a bit hard. I knew that by the time that I got to Nashville, all of the stores and shops would be closed. And with my flight leaving super early in the morning, that night was my last chance at finding something. I could sense feelings of discouragement beginning to rise up within me. It wasn't about not having glasses; it was more so the act of putting a ton of hope and faith in God and feeling like it just wasn't going to happen. I talked with God throughout the drive, trying to arrive at a place of rest in my heart. I had seen Him come through so mightily with Oscar, that a part of me began to see what a life of being God's best friend *could* look like. But as I sat there fighting off feelings of discouragement, I couldn't help but prepare myself for a letdown.

After going back and forth with God, I began to feel like He was going to bring the glasses to me and that I didn't need to go and buy any for myself. I found myself whispering out loud as I drove down the freeway, "I will trust you. I will trust you, God." — And this is how I know God is *super* patient. Right after I said, "I will trust you", I saw a grocery store on the side of the road, so I quickly stopped in to see if they had any glasses, which they of course were sold out. I walked back to the car saying, "Ok, now we're doing the trust thing, *sorry*, my bad."

As I arrived in Nashville, I was super tired from driving around all day, and I wanted nothing more than to just relax at the hotel. But when I arrived at the hotel that my GPS took me to, the guy at the front desk told me I was at the wrong hotel. He pointed to one down the street and said the address that I wanted was right there. So I got back in my car and drove to the next one, only to be told the exact same thing again. The lady at the front desk of the second hotel pointed back down the other end of the street and said that the address I was looking for was over there. I didn't know the name of the hotel that I was looking for because Louise had booked it online and sent me only the address. So I got back in my car again and drove to the third hotel. I walked in and gave them my info, only to be told a third time that I was still at the wrong hotel. At this point, I wanted to say, "Forget it! I'm just gonna sleep in the car." There was still a battle of discouragement going on inside of me, and on the outside, I had to deal with the Hotel Liars Society. The guy at the latest hotel could tell that I was tired and frustrated. He gently leaned over the front desk and spoke in a super soft voice, *"Alright, let's figure this out, OK?"* Something in his voice made me feel better like he had all the answers.

He pulled up all the hotels on the street and located the *actual* correct one. He gave me a very detailed description of how to get there and shook my hand. I said thank you so so much and started to walk away, but then I stopped, and turned around back at him and said, "You wouldn't happen to have any of those Solar Eclipse glasses would you?" He looked back at me as a smile began to spread across his face. Without saying anything, he walked over to another desk and reached behind it, and pulled out a brand new pair of Eclipse glasses. "Here, you can have these." He said nonchalantly. I just stood there, staring at the glasses in my hand like I was holding the golden ticket in Charlie and the Chocolate Factory. "YOU HAVE NO IDEA HOW HARD I WAS LOOKING FOR GLASSES?" I screamed. He just smiled and said, "You're welcome."

I drove back to the hotel in silence. I don't know why, but in those moments, I don't often get very loud or animated. I get very quiet. The only things I could say were *wow* and *thank you*. That day had so many ups and downs. So many confusing moments. So many twists and turns. Newton Street, all the wrong hotels, etc. And it all started off with something that seemed so insignificant as well; just getting some Eclipse glasses. But the more I opened myself up to the possibility that God really cared about the *little things* in my life like a *best friend* would, the more I found old fears that needed to be dealt with. But there I was, sitting front row at 39,000 feet the very next day. Wearing a pair of glasses that were birthed out of pain, out of process, out of His presence. To someone else, getting a pair of glasses may have seemed like the smallest thing in the world, but to me, it spoke volumes. And as I looked out of the window, I realized that even the *little* things in life could be testimonies of transformation if we let them.

CHAPTER 16

THE 'WHOLE' CHURCH

As I got home from my latest trip, I began to ponder how the Lord kept on creating ways to show me how much He cared for me as a *friend*. And as I thought about that, an interesting thought popped into my head, "What little things do *you* care about God?" He had been doing so many things for me lately, that I started to wonder what stuff God Himself was into. What came from that was not what I expected.

Out of nowhere, I started getting the sudden urge to visit every church in Redding. I tried to ignore it at first, but it stuck in my mind for weeks, and I couldn't stop thinking about it. It was the strangest thing. So one day, I decided to Google how many churches were actually in Redding, and I was shocked to see there were about a hundred different churches. I shouted out, "There's no way I can visit all of those churches! And I'm not even sure why I want to. This is crazy!" But the thought kept coming to me over and over. After trying to ignore it for what seemed like months, I began to realize that maybe God was trying to show me something. So one Sunday morning, I decided to take a giant leap of faith and attend a random church by myself that I had never been to before.

I pulled up a list of churches and chose one at random. It was called Risen King. I had no idea what this was all about; I just knew I needed to do it. I arrived at the church, but since I didn't know anybody, I sat down quietly by myself in the back. The pastor grabbed the microphone and began to share about how he felt that they were to pray for physical healing that Sunday morning. He went on to say that they don't usually do that very often. So the pastor stood up there alone and asked people to come forward. I thought to myself, "Oh! I bet that's why I'm here! Maybe I can go up there and help pray for people's healing along with the pastor." As I thought that, the Lord immediately interrupted me, *"I don't want you to pray for anyone here. That's not why I brought you here. I brought you here to see a different side of my heart that you haven't experienced yet."* Just then, a scripture popped into my mind; *Romans 12*. I didn't know what the scripture was off the top of my head, so I pulled out my bible.

ROMANS 12: 2-17

Do not conform to the pattern of this world, but be transformed by the renewing of your mind. Then you will be able to test and approve what God's will is—his good, pleasing and perfect will.

For by the grace given me I say to every one of you: Do not think of yourself more highly than you ought, but rather think of yourself with sober judgment, in accordance with the faith God has distributed to each of you. For just as each of us has one body with many members, and these members do not all have the same function, so in Christ we, though many, form one body, and each member belongs to all the others. We have different gifts, according to the grace given to each of us. If your gift is prophesying, then prophesy in accordance with your faith; if it is serving, then serve; if it is teaching, then teach; if it is to encourage, then give encouragement; if it is giving, then give generously; if it is to lead, do it diligently; if it is to show mercy, do it cheerfully.

Love must be sincere. Hate what is evil; cling to what is good. Be devoted to one another in love. Honor one another above yourselves. Never be lacking in zeal, but keep your spiritual fervor, serving the Lord. Be joyful in hope, patient in affliction, faithful in prayer. Share with the Lord's people who are in need. Practice hospitality.

Bless those who persecute you; bless and do not curse. Rejoice with those who rejoice; mourn with those who mourn. Live in harmony with one another. Do not be proud, but be willing to associate with people of low position. Do not be conceited.

Do not repay anyone evil for evil. Be careful to do what is right in the eyes of everyone. If it is possible, as far as it depends on you, live at peace with everyone.

I read this scripture silently to myself. But as I came to the end, I heard Holy Spirit say, *"You're not here to give, you're here to receive. Every church carries a different part of my heart. None is more important than the others."* I looked back at the scripture; it's words seemed to jump off the page — 'one body with many members'. He continued on, *"If you can learn to find the different parts of who I am within every church, then there is no place that I can't take you."* As I sat there, a realization began to sink in: some churches may do hospitality really well, some may have a huge heart for the lost, some may have an incredible understanding of what healthy family looks like. I started to think about all the different types of churches in Redding. There were Baptists churches, Evangelical churches, Catholic churches, Nazarene churches, Vineyard churches, Presbyterian churches, Methodist churches, Anglican churches, other churches that I hadn't even heard of! But a lot of them were a night and day difference from Bethel. And some of them, I knew for a fact, had radically different beliefs than I did. What if they didn't believe in miracles? What if they don't believe God is good? What if they don't value honour? What if they have no passion?! I began to judge them in my heart.

The words from the scripture drifted back towards me, *'one body with many members'*, and the Lord said, *"If you judge them, Gabriel, you judge me."* I felt so convicted. Even if I can only see 1% of God in some of these places, 1% still means that God is present! And 1% of God is more precious than every other treasure. How could I not honour what the King of the universe deems as important? There is a treasure trove of blessings hidden within the hearts of Christians spreading across every denomination. But I knew the only way that I could access that blessing was to humble myself in order to receive from them. I couldn't just live life drawing from what was familiar to me. God began to speak again, *The only prayer I want you to pray within these churches is this: I pray that this church would come into the original destiny that God has always planned for it.* So I closed my bible and prayed just that. I prayed that whatever Risen King's original destiny looked like, that whatever it's unique purpose was, that it would come into a complete fullness in Jesus name.

At this point in the service, the worship team had come on stage to play. I sat there and watched as hundreds of Christians worshipped Jesus together as one. It was interesting to think that on any given Sunday, there were probably thousands of Christians across the city of Redding worshipping Jesus at the same time and not even knowing it. As I sat watching, God ever so gently began to place His finger on a mindset that I didn't realize I had. And the more He did, the more a conviction started to settle in my heart. I bowed my head and whispered, "Lord, forgive me for thinking that Bethel was the only reason that you have blessed this city. Forgive me for thinking that we were the only ones taking steps to transform this city. Every Sunday, Christians across the city have filled their home churches and worshipped you for years. Forgive me for being so arrogant to think that Redding's breakthrough would come from only us." As I prayed that out, a soft peace came over me.

I stood up after that prayer and began to worship along with them. Risen King and Bethel Church are similar in a lot of ways, so it wasn't difficult for me to engage. Revelations of what that church carried began to flow over my mind. My heart was instantly filled! I was so appreciative of my new brothers and sisters, so grateful for who they are in Christ and what they add to the body. It was different than what I was used to but beautifully unique! *And equally important.* I set in my heart right then and there to visit every church in Redding. I knew that some of them may not always be as easy for me as that first one was. I knew there would be times where I might have to really humble myself in order to receive from them. But I loved the fact that when I asked God about the little things He enjoyed in life, His answer was about family.

I didn't fully understand why I was on that journey; I just knew God liked it. And as of this writing, I still haven't visited them all. But I will tell you this – over the years I have attended many vastly different churches all across my city, and it has been one of the most exciting and challenging *(and fruitful)* experiences of my entire life. God has brought me to just the right church on just the right Sunday so many times. Each church carried a uniquely different part of God's heart, some that I had never felt before. And just like with any God adventure, some very interesting things have happened along the way. One time I attended an incredible homeless church outside of a Mc-Donalds. One time a church asked me to be a part of their worship team. One church that I attended ended up inviting me to a wedding reception they were having afterward *(I sat with them and enjoyed ice cream Sundays)*. One church was so hard to receive from that it triggered me to the point that I actually walked out early without receiving anything at all. It took me about two years before I could finally return to receive from them.

I want to say this as well: Bethel will always be my home church. I firmly believe in the culture of honour that we carry. That DNA will always flow in my heart through and through. And I didn't start this crazy adventure because Bethel was missing something. I believe the Lord set me on this personal journey to simply learn one thing: *to love fully when you don't agree completely.* I still attend Bethel services when possible, while at the same time balancing my attending of new churches. I honestly don't know how long it will take me to visit them all. And with my travel schedule, it takes even longer. But growing up in the church, I often only saw one side of God. And while it was beautiful, I began to discover that each church carries a different unique revelation of God's character. Every church I visited seemed to add more and more to the shape of His personality, and as I came home every Sunday afternoon, I was constantly filled with the desire to discover even more. Even if it takes me a lifetime, it will be a life well spent.

Going to all of these churches has been an incredible adventure. And like I said, I'm still on the journey. I could write chapters and chapters from the different things I've discovered about God's personality over the years. And to be honest, someday I hope to tell the complete story of that adventure and what God has shown me through it. But as I witnessed the different aspects of God that I had never seen before, I was brought to a place where I desired more than ever to have a *friend* like Jesus.

CHAPTER 17

BEHIND THE NAME

There are times in your life where something so dramatic happens that you remember every detail of the day as if you were reading it from a book. I'll never forget this next story for as long as I live. Heidi Baker was visiting Redding and she was going to preach at Bethel. I had already gone through all of BSSM, but I wasn't going to miss out on hearing Heidi speak. She had such an impact on me during my time in Mozambique. And every time I heard her preach, something amazing always happened.

During her sermon, she began to talk about the power of our destiny and calling within the kingdom. Everyone in the room was sitting on the edge of their seats, hanging onto every single word. Around me were groups of people on their knees, weeping and wailing throughout her sermon. Eventually, they got so stirred up that they rushed the front for prayer without hesitation. *Typical* Heidi Baker service. But as much as I tried to connect and engage with what she was sharing, I couldn't. I had other things on my mind. For some reason during the service, I couldn't stop thinking about Stephen and Kevin. I didn't know why all these feelings started resurfacing out of no where. Sometimes the worst thing about grief is our inability to *choose* when it happens. I tried my best to ignore it so I could pay attention to what she was talking about, but it seemed that the longer she spoke, the deeper I sank.

Eventually, I had to step out of the room in the middle of her sermon. More feelings were starting to come up that I hadn't felt in years. I started getting so frustrated at myself. "Why is this happening now? I don't want to feel these things!" I had to get in my car and drive home. I was hoping that by leaving the church, I would get out from under that cloud. But now that I was alone, the grief seemed to swallow me whole. I began to weep out loud in the car -- hard. I started to remember individual stories of how loyal my friends were to me. And the fact that I didn't have *that* loyal friend in my life anymore killed me. I screamed out, "They're not here anymore, God! So what are you gonna do?! You have to be THAT loyal to me, God! You have to be that loyal friend that I don't have anymore! You have to fill what I don't have anymore! If you really wanna be my best friend, then you have to be what I lost!" All the pain and frustration that I had been holding back for years came flooding to the surface. After I screamed those last few words in the car, it got quiet, dead silent. There were no more tears. Just *pain*.

A few minutes later, I pulled up to my house and went inside. I hadn't said anything more to God since that last outburst. To be honest, I didn't know what else to say. I sat on my bed, still not saying a word. I laid there for a few minutes just staring at the ceiling. I didn't want to speak at all. It's not that I didn't have anything to say, I just didn't want to talk. And for some reason, God hadn't said one word to me about anything so far. I was frustrated, but I was in more pain than frustration. And without meaning to, I felt the words slip out of my mouth, "Please be that friend to me, Jesus." Just then, Oscar jumped up on my bed and started licking my face ravenously. I was totally taken by surprise and didn't see him coming. I tried pushing him off me, but his licks kept coming. I was really not in the mood to play, so I pushed him off my face with a stern, "Stop it!" He sort of looked at me for a moment with a puzzled gaze, then jumped off the bed and towards the kitchen. I sat there a bit jumbled for a second, then slowly looked back towards the ceiling as if readdressing God. But just as I was about to open my mouth to speak, I heard Oscar bark loudly from the kitchen. And as soon as he barked, I heard the Lord say to me loud and clear, *"Look up Oscar's name because that's who I am to you and that's why I brought him into your life."*

I was stunned by God's response. I had no idea what the name, *Oscar*, meant. So I pulled out my phone and typed it into Google. This is what it said: The name Oscar is derived from a warrior in Irish mythology that was known for befriending deer. The Gaelic word "os" means deer and "cara" means friend. So the name 'Oscar' literally translates into 'Deer Friend.' When I read those words out loud, I heard the Lord say, *"Gabriel, I'm your Dear Friend."*

I laid there quietly on my bed, completely speechless. I had always loved God so deeply, but after my friends passed away, I kept Him at arm's length in the category of my *best friend*. There was just too much pain in that spot. But He never pushed it any further when I said no, He just waited. Waited for me. I sat up in my bed and stared out into the empty room. I took a deep breath and whispered these words, "Alright, God. Let's do this. You can be my best friend; you can be my *dear friend.*"

And I sat there on my bed, dwelling on my new found friendship, something dawned on me. Two years before that I had stayed up late asking God for a prophetic word from Shawn Bolz, only to be told that Oscar was going to bring healing to our family. But what I never saw coming was that the healing would actually be for me. And that out of all the words given that day, I had been given the most precious one of all. I was hoping for a quick prophetic word to make me feel good, but God wanted to give me something so much more than that. He gave His hand in friendship and the journey that followed it. As I look back on that day where my pain chose to resurface, I don't remember it as a day of grief. It will be forever marked in my mind as something else entirely.

I remember it as the day I finally said yes.

I remember it as the day where I finally stopped running.

And I remember it as the day where I finally became *best friends* with God.

CHAPTER 18

WHO'S COUNTING?

Accepting God's invitation to be best friends was one of the hardest journey's I've ever been on. But after saying yes, there was a part of my heart that finally felt at peace. I had always loved the Lord, but in the depths of my soul, I was holding back; holding back because of what I had lost. And because of that, I could never fully escape that *loneliness*. God had become my best friend, and with that came more freedom than I could have possibly imagined. But even after all that, there was still one more thing that terrified me. *The fear of death*. But my new best friend wouldn't allow me to be afraid forever.

One day I was at home working on my computer when I got a text from my mom. The text read: "Your father is having chest pains. Taking him to the hospital." When I read those words, I felt paralyzed with fear. Both my grandparents had heart attacks and triple bypass surgeries when they were alive. And my entire life, my dad had chest pains from time to time. Growing up I always just assumed he would be fine, but after Stephen and Kevin died, I laid awake at night thinking about it sometimes. Louise asked me what was wrong, but I couldn't speak. My dad never went to the hospital for anything. I knew it was serious. The only thing I could say was, "We need to go to the hospital right now."

We only lived a few minutes away from the hospital, but the drive felt like an eternity. As much as I tried not thinking of the worst case scenario, my thoughts began to slip into scary places. Louise and I arrived at the hospital and immediately saw my mom waiting for us. She said the doctors were doing tests on my dad to see what happened to him and that all we could do was sit and wait in the meantime. Waiting rooms could not be more appropriately named. You sit amongst total strangers, but it doesn't matter if some of them are lawyers, janitors, teachers, whatever, because in that waiting room, you're all the same. Is it going to be good news? Is it going to be bad news? No one knows. All that's left is waiting; waiting in that *terrible* silence.

It was about 2 AM when the doctor came walking in. I immediately stood up; I had been trying to fall asleep, but it was no use. I started searching for the right words to ask him what happened, but before I could open my mouth, the doctor said in the most unsympathetic way, "Well, looks like he had a heart attack." It caught me off-guard. My mom stared at him with a puzzled look on her face and said, "He.. he had a heart attack?" The doctor's tone hadn't improved, "Yup, that's what I said. Heart attack." It got quiet for a moment as we tried taking in the news we had just heard. Then my mom asked, "Well, what, what happens now?" The doctor wiped his eyes as he looked at his clip-board, "Well we'll open him up and put some stents in him. One of his arteries is 70% closed, and the other is 85%. So we'll see what we can do." I could tell my mom was annoyed by his tactless demeanor, but not wanting to get on his bad side, she thanked him, and our waiting continued.

A few hours later, a nurse came out and said that we could go in and see my dad now. Walking in and see my father in a hospital bed was hard to see, but I didn't let myself cry. I didn't want to *feel* emotion at that moment. If I were to let myself feel, then who knows how far I would fall into that pit of pain. The fear of death had made me numb. I hugged my dad as we waited for the doctor to return with the results. He finally came back in and said that they were able to put a stent in the 85% blocked artery, but not the 70% one. His explanation of the surgery was just as crass as when we first talked to him. We thanked him as he left and turned back towards my dad. I could see tears formed in the corner of my dad's eyes. "This wasn't supposed to happen." He said in a whisper. When he said those words, it almost broke me. But I pushed that emotion away; further down. The nurse then informed us that it was time for my dad to get some rest. I looked over at my dad and said, "I'm gonna drop Louise off at the house really quick, but then I will be right back. Ok?" My dad gave me a soft nod with his head. I immediately turned to the door and walked out. I had to get out of that room as fast as I could. I could feel myself beginning to break. I could feel it rising up.

As Louise and I got into our car, I began to put the key in the ignition, when I suddenly stopped. Louise looked at me and asked, "What's wrong?" I didn't answer her. I just set the keys down and stared out the front window of the car. I couldn't take it anymore. The fear of death gripped my entire body. I started having terrible thoughts going through my mind, "He's going to die. Just admit it. Just come to terms with it. He's going to die. Just accept it." Everything inside of me wanted to give up and agree with those words. But as I had those thoughts, I could feel God tugging at my heart just as hard saying, *"Speak life, Gabriel."* I closed my eyes and clenched my teeth. I could feel the battle between both worlds. I wanted to accept defeat so bad at that moment. I wanted to say that I was no match for death. But something inside of me knew that if I were to partner with those words, that my dad would die that night.

It felt like my brain was being torn in two. I began to scream out as the struggle waged like a storm in my head. I reached out and grabbed the steering wheel as hard as I could to help endure the battle. I couldn't last any longer; I was about to give up, when out of nowhere, I heard a faint voice piercing through the cloud saying, *"I will trust you. I will trust you. I will trust you."* It startled me when I heard it, but what surprised me even more, is that the voice that I was hearing was actually *mine*. I leaned forward in my seat as if trying to get closer to the source. It started to get louder, *"I will trust you. I will trust you. I will trust you."* I couldn't understand why I was hearing my own voice saying that. I thought about it for a moment, then decided to say those words on my own. I began to speak out loud, "I will trust you. I will trust you. I will trust you." As I said those words, I began to feel the winds of that storm start to die down. I started saying it louder, "I will trust you. I will trust you. I will trust you, God." The weight of that fear began to lift off of me until I couldn't feel it at all. I opened my eyes and looked around. I noticed Louise was still sitting in the passenger seat with a look on her face that said, "Um, what the heck is happening to you?" I kept looking around the car, waiting to see if that feeling of fear would return, but it didn't. My eyes drifted up to the hospital as I looked out towards my dad. A smile spread across my face as I said, "I have to get back here. I have to get back for him." I quickly put the keys into the ignition and took off towards our house. Louise looked at me and said, "Are you ok, Sweetie?" I didn't answer right away. All I could do was stare out the window with a smile and say, "It's finally gone. I'm free. I'm free."

I'll never forget the calm that I felt as I watched over my dad for the rest of the night. I stayed up till about 6 AM just watching him sleep. He had tubes and IV's and all sorts of things coming out of him; but as I sat there listening to those beeping monitors, I felt no fear at all. Death had lost its sting. As I looked back on the night, I started to realize why it was my own voice that I heard in the car. I needed to be the one to stand against that fear. No one else could do it for me. That fear tried to make me feel like a victim, but what I carried inside of me was greater than any darkness, and I needed to let it out. Whatever hold it had over me was broken. I knew that my *best friend* was going to protect my dad. It honestly felt as if the peace of God had enclosed itself tightly around that hospital room, and not even death itself could find a way through. I didn't know what the future held; I just knew God was going to carry us through to victory.

The next day, the doctor came in to see how my dad was doing. I decided to leave the room for a second to go to the bathroom. But when I returned, I heard the doctor saying to my dad, "What? You don't have insurance? You guys are screwed! You're gonna lose your home!" He started arguing with my dad before eventually walking out. I looked at my mom and asked what just happened. She let out a deep breath and said, "Because I worked in education for 31 years, I've always had insurance. And we've never needed it once. But it just recently expired, and we've been without insurance for two weeks as we were about to renew it. But unfortunately, your father's heart attack won't be covered." I couldn't believe it. They had insurance for 31 years, and then during a two-week timespan that they were renewing it, my dad had a heart attack. But what was even more shocking than that was the doctor's response. I couldn't believe he said those things to a man who had just had a heart attack! It felt like a total word curse. And my parents weren't having any part of it. They immediately took a stance in prayer against what the doctor had said about losing their home. My dad spent a total of four days in the hospital. So how much does a four-day stay rack up in charges for someone with no insurance you might ask? A whopping bill of over $170,000. And before we knew it, people from the hospital were calling in to make sure they collected every single penny of it.

My parents are prayer warriors at heart; they always have been. If they see some an injustice in life, they will pray with fiery passion until it shifts. But after dealing with a heart attack and now the fear of possibly losing their home, they were spread thin. One night we were at their house when my dad turned to me and asked Louise and I to pray for them. I could see the tiredness on their faces -- the weariness of the season. I put my hands on their shoulders and began to pray. I half expected God to fill them with zeal and energy to stand victorious, but something else happened instead. As I waited on God to speak, I felt Him say one word, *"Rest."* I said to them, "I feel like God is saying that you need to rest. That it would take more faith for you not to pray fervently, and just to rest in the fact that God will take care of everything." My parents thanked us for praying and gave us hugs. I could tell they were still feeling the weight of the situation on their shoulders. Resting wasn't always their *go-to,* but in a season where they had nothing left to give, they chose to rest in faith. And later that week, my dad had a dream.

In the dream, my dad heard a soft voice say to him, *"Mr. Lopez, we're going to cancel your debt."* When he heard that voice, he suddenly woke up. My dad rarely has dreams, so when he does, he knows they're significant. A few days after the dream, he got another phone call from the hospital. For weeks he had been getting nasty phone calls day and night from people trying to collect money from him, but this time was different. He answered the phone hesitantly, but to his surprise, on the other end was a sweet lady that he had never spoken with before. A soft voice came through the phone, "Hello there, am I speaking to Juan?" My dad told her that she was. The lady continued, "Well, I am calling to talk to you about your recent bill, and, well, Mr. Lopez, we're going to cancel your debt." My dad sat up in his chair, holding the phone as close to his face as possible, "Excuse me. I'm sorry. What did you just say?" He blurted out. She repeated herself, "I said we're going to cancel your debt, Mr. Lopez." And just like that, their $170,000 debt was wiped completely clean.

Actually, it was $171,249 to be exact, but who's counting?

My *best friend* was counting, that's who.

God never ceases to amaze me. Sometimes the term life changing can be used too often, but in this instance, it's an understatement. What the devil meant for bad, God turned around for His glory. And in that process, He delivered me from a fear that had held me captive for many years. And you know what makes me so happy to think about? Since having that heart attack, my dad has changed his whole diet and is eating incredibly healthy. And the artery that was once 70% closed in his heart, has now opened up significantly and continues to do so. I will never forget what God did for our family, and I will never forget what He did for me.

"Where, O death, is your victory? Where, O death, is your sting?"
1 Corinthians 15:55

CHAPTER 19

THE HOLY LAND

From the outset of this book, two things were significant to me: writing about my trip to Israel with Welton Academy and launching the book on my 30th birthday. But what makes it challenging is that my trip to Israel was ending on March 19th and my birthday was on March 24th. So a week out from launching my book, I had absolutely no idea where the story would go or how it would conclude. I'm not going to lie; there was a small part of me that was terrified that nothing would happen and that I wouldn't have a final chapter. But there was an even bigger part of me that wanted to end on the ultimate adventure. And just like Jesus called for Peter to step out of the boat, I could feel God calling my name as well. This book is a *journey of trust*, so let's step out on the water together.

On the plane to Tel Aviv, there was a family with four little girls sitting in front of Louise and I. As we were about to land, I noticed the dad turn around and smile at his little girls as they woke up one by one. I thought to myself, "He seems like a good father." And as I thought that, the little girls started saying, *"Abba! Abba!"* Which in Hebrew means *father*. When you grow up in the church, you hear countless worship songs declaring God as *Abba Father*. Which also at that moment made me realize how we've basically just been saying *Father Father* the whole time. But as I listened to the little girls call out to their dad with precious smiles on their faces, it dawned on me that

I was about to step into a land that was utterly foreign to me in every way.

One of the first sites that we visited was the place where Mary Magdalene was born, called Magdala. There were blocks of stone and scattered ruins everywhere. Coming from America, it's hard to fathom just how ancient these spots are. It's one thing to hear the word *old*, but it's another thing when you see cities built upon cities that were built upon even older cities. There were often times that we had to climb down 40 to 50 feet just to get to the original buildings. Rain and mud had entirely covered the older towns over time, and so new cities were built on top of them. Our tour guide led us to the town synagogue in Magdala and showed us what a typical service would have looked like. She pointed over to a seat in the center of the synagogue and said, "Jesus would have sat in a seat just like that as He read Isaiah 61." She opened her bible and read Jesus' words.

"The Spirit of the Lord is upon me,
because he has anointed me
to proclaim good news to the poor.
He has sent me to proclaim liberty to the captives
and recovering of sight to the blind,
to set at liberty those who are oppressed,
to proclaim the year of the Lord's favor."

She went on to say, "Imagine every eye fixed on Jesus at that moment. And Him looking back at them with His piercing gaze." I looked around the synagogue and imagined what it must have been like to hear Jesus read that passage. Maybe some were in awe; maybe some were offended. As I stood there staring over the ancient ruins, I could almost see the expressions on their faces and the stirring of the crowd. And as my eyes drifted back to the center of the room, a single white feather fell from the air and landed on the seat.

From there we visited the site where the angel Gabriel told Mary that she would give birth to Jesus. Often there would be a place of worship or church built on or around an old biblical site. As we walked into the church that was built there, I couldn't help but notice all of the beautiful designs on the walls and ceilings. The artwork was hundreds of years old from all sorts of people who had settled there after the time of Jesus. Golden ornaments were hanging from the ceiling, priceless tapestries on all of the walls, and candles that led down to the place where Mary saw Gabriel. As we got closer to the bottom, I realized there was fence blocking off the area where they believed the encounter took place. I walked up and put my face against the metal bars as I peered around the dark room. It was such a simple place. There was an entire building above that was adorned with stunning decorations from top to bottom; all of this for a simple little place below. I thought to myself, "I wonder what Mary must have felt in that dark little room all by herself." But my thought was quickly interrupted as I noticed a crowd forming behind me waiting to view the room. As much as I didn't want to, I decided to continue forward up the stairs so other people could have a chance to see it as well. But as I walked up the steps, I started feeling something very strange.

My whole body started to get very hot, and I instantly started to sweat. I was confused because it had been cool the entire time before that. When I got to the top of the stairs, I noticed the rest of the Welton Academy team sitting in on a church service. I tried to walk over to the pews to take a seat, but it seemed the more that I walked, the stranger I felt. My whole body started trembling, and I honestly felt like I was going to pass out. I could feel the *fear of the Lord* around me like a thick cloud. I set my camera down and knelt by some chairs to try to gather myself. A few minutes later, the feeling started to subside, and it was time to go to the Sea of Galilee. As I carefully picked myself off the floor, I wondered what it was that I had felt. At the time I had no clue, but as I sat here writing this, I suddenly remembered what I had said to myself right before it happened. *"I wonder what Mary must have felt in that dark little room all by herself."* I'm glad I only felt a glimpse of that moment. Now it makes sense why the angel Gabriel said, *"Mary, don't be afraid."*

All throughout the gospels, you hear about the Sea of Galilee. But if you're anything like me, it's hard to visualize scriptures without seeing it with your own eyes. So I was excited to hear that we were going on a boat ride over the Sea of Galilee. Our team climbed onto a massive barge, and we set sail out into open waters. It was a beautiful day outside: clear sky's, birds overhead, and the sound of the water splashing against the wooden hull; creating a gentle mist that you could feel on your skin. I made my way to the front of the boat and hung my legs off the edge. I looked out to sea and watched as the orange sun was just setting over the calm waters. I imagined what it must have been like to fish there thousands of years ago; struggling to pull in a fresh catch into their tiny wooden boats. I imagined what it must have been like to see Jesus walking on the water in the midst of a storm. To hear Him call out to me, just like He did with Peter. *"Come."* I looked below and imagined what Peter must have felt as he stepped out onto the water as the capsizing waves crashed against their fragile boat. Those first few steps must have been shaky, like a toddler struggling to stay standing as they make their way towards their father. With so much of Jesus' life taking place at the Sea of Galilee, it felt as if the bible was coming to life right in front of my eyes. It was incredible to see those different stories over the water as we sailed, that is until I heard a voice over the loudspeaker from the back of the boat say, "Hey you, at the front, please keep your legs in the boat at all times. Thank you." -- Moment over.

One thing I never expected in my life was to see the Jordan River where Jesus was baptized. But even less than that was the idea that I would ever get baptized there myself. When we got out of the bus, I noticed there were crowds of people congregating near the bank of the Jordan River. If the Sea of Galilee was bigger than I expected, the Jordan River was much smaller. When I made my way down to the bottom, I saw people with white robes getting baptized. I went to put my feet in the water when I overheard that some of the people from our group were going to buy robes to get baptized as well. They looked at me and asked if I wanted to come. I had already been baptized before, so I wasn't planning on getting baptized again, but when I suddenly realized that this was a once in a lifetime opportunity, I screamed, "Let's do it!" And so I went and bought myself one of those fancy robes, too.

I returned to the river to see Jonathan and a few others in the water already baptizing some members of our group. When I stepped down into the murky water, I had to stop and gather myself because it was so cold. I hate being cold. Hate it. Loathe it actually. The only ocean I've ever enjoyed was the one in Hawaii because it felt like bath water. When you're as skinny as me, it takes about two seconds for the cold to reach your heart and for your teeth to start chattering. So when I stepped into the river, I shot a quick glance towards heaven and said under my breath, "I'm doing this for my best friend." I made my way down into the river and was met by the three members of the group who were baptizing people (Matthew, Mark, and Jon). *So close to having all the four gospel guys.* They gathered around me while Jon said a prayer over my future. It was awesome to think how much Jonathan had so impacted my life, to the point of baptizing me in the Jordan River. Once Jonathan had finished praying, Mark placed his hand on my chest and quickly dunked me under the cold water. I'm not sure if it was the Holy Spirit or just the freezing cold, but when I came out of the water, I felt more alive than I ever have. As I looked out over the tall reeds that sprouted out from the water, I couldn't feel the cold anymore. I didn't cry, or scream, I just stood there in the water, speechless. I gently placed my hands across the top of the flowing river; feeling the current pushing underneath my fingers. For the first time since being in Israel, I suddenly realized why God had brought me there. Jesus had been with me during my entire journey so far. He was with me in the restaurants in Lakeland, Florida. He was with me on the streets of Mexico City. And he was with me in bush bush of Mozambique. But Jesus brought me to Israel for a different reason; He brought me there so I could see where *He* grew up. To see the streets that *He* walked on. But not just to *see* it, to *experience* it firsthand. I looked down at the same water that my best friend had been baptized in over 2000 years ago. All I could do was smile. And to throw some extra *super-spiritual-comedy* on the side, as I stood there looking out at the river, someone from behind me yelled, "Look up there!" And just above our heads flew a single *white dove*. I guess God likes the *classics*.

The next day we went to Bethlehem, the birthplace of Jesus. I couldn't wait to continue with this new perspective of seeing the places where my best friend grew up. There was a massive church built on top of the spot where Mary gave birth to Jesus. As you walk in, there is a huge hall with pillars as tall as two-story buildings. Along the walls of the church, there were enormous white sheets of paper that spread all the way across for people to write on as they wait in line to go underground. I could tell that as one paper had been filled, it was moved up the wall and replaced by another sheet of paper beneath it. There were so many filled in sheets of paper that went way up to the top of the room. All of them covered in writing from top to bottom. I moved in closer so I could read the ones that were near the floor level. I was stunned at how many people poured their hearts out to Jesus as they recounted what He had done in their lives. Some people wrote about how He had been faithful to heal them, others how He protected their family, and there were some that just felt deeply loved in their time of need. I wish I had a pen on me at that moment. I would have written about friendship with God. But as I stood there staring at their stories, it dawned on me that God was the *answer* to every single one of their problems. Those that needed healing; He touched their bodies. Those that needed financial provision; He blessed them abundantly. Those that needed deliverance; He freed them from darkness. There were so many needs, so many diverse problems, but the *solution* was always the same. Their journeys had been tough, but I could see God calling out to each and every one of them in the midst of their pain, saying *"I will be your best friend."* Just for fun, I want to list the countries below that I was able to write down while waiting in line. Maybe your country is there. If not, then perhaps one day you can be the one to write it down yourself.

Indonesia, Mexico, Ecuador, United States, Columbia, Turkey, Guam, Romania, Poland, Tonga, Philippines, Kenya, Peru, Spain, Ukraine, France, Guatemala, India, Canada, Australia, Croatia, Brazil, Sweden, Singapore, Chile, Cuba, China, and so many more that I couldn't keep up.

As we finally made our way through the waiting area, we came upon a narrow door that led to where Jesus was born. It took some time for people to get through because the crowd was so big and the door was so small, but as we entered, we stumbled upon the spot where Mary had given birth. There is a large silver star of David on the floor that marks the actual place. When it was my turn to see, I set down my camera and laid out flat directly on it. I imagined what it must have been like to give birth in a cold dark cave like that. I wondered if Joseph felt helpless as he watched Mary scream from her labor; and what they felt inside as Jesus took His first tiny breaths on His own. I didn't care if people were watching; I leaned forward and kissed the ground under my face. This is where it all started. This is where all of Heaven had its gaze fixed on one single child: my best friend. I felt as if I was watching a movie of Jesus' entire childhood in intimate detail. But as beautiful as these moments were in the life of Christ, there were hardships ahead as well.

I'll never forget the Garden of Gethsemane. So far nothing had been like what I pictured in my head while growing up. But the Garden of Gethsemane was different. It was exactly as I imagined it. I could see why Jesus chose to pray there often. It was secluded and yet inviting all at the same time. The trees throughout the garden had a mysterious look to them. Their trunks were short in height but wide in width, and their branches hung low creating a *cave-like* feeling under each tree. Just inside the building that connected to the garden was a place called the Rock of Agony. It was the spot where Jesus fell to the ground in anguish, moments before being betrayed. As you walk in you can see the massive slab of stone still there. Crowds of people were all around the rock reaching their hand out and touching it as they prayed. I knelt down and put both of my hands on the rock, but when I did, I began to feel a deep sadness. I immediately wanted to pull my hands away, but something kept me there. As strange as it sounds, it felt like I was comforting Jesus in the garden by staying there. I slowly ran my hands across the surface of the dirty rock as I whispered, *"I'm here, my friend. I'm here."* And the longer I held my hands there; the clearer I could see Jesus praying in the garden. After a while, I felt someone tapping me on my shoulder. I ignored at first, but the tapping persisted. I picked up my head to see Louise pointing at the door while saying, "We have to go, Babe." I paused for a moment, and then glanced around to see that I was completely by myself; everyone had left. It's one thing to hear about Jesus being betrayed in the garden, but when you *feel* the rock that He wept on while His disciples slept nearby, it all suddenly becomes real. I felt like I carried that sadness around with me for a few days. I just couldn't shake it for some reason. But on the last night of our trip, everything finally made sense.

It was our last night, and we were going to the site of Jesus' crucifixion and burial tomb. Our tour guide led us to the spot where Jesus was crucified, called Golgotha, which means *Place of the Skull*. It was interesting to look up see the face of a skull protruding from out of the side of a rock face. But I'm not going to lie; I didn't want to *imagine* what the crucifixion would have looked like for Jesus. Maybe it was because I was still feeling heavy from the Rock of Agony -- I don't know. Whatever it was, I didn't spend too much time at Golgotha. But as the tour guide continued on, leading us to the burial site of Jesus, I stepped inside to see the empty tomb with my own eyes. I looked around the small room and then back at the door again. The stone that the Romans were ordered to seal the tomb with would have been enormous. Impossible for a group of fishermen to move on their own; let alone getting past the trained Roman soldiers to do it. But as I looked at the wall next to the door, I noticed a sign hanging there that read:

*"HE IS NOT HERE -
FOR HE IS RISEN."*

As I sat stood there staring at the sign, I couldn't move. I had heard this phrase countless times in my life. I've even said it many times myself. But when I stood there in that empty tomb, I finally *understood* something. When Jesus rose from that place, there was no more sadness, only victory. I began to think about all of the problems that were written on those white sheets of paper where Jesus was born. The only reason Jesus was the solution to all of that pain was that He was the only one with the authority to do anything about it. *Lack* — conquered. *Rejection* – conquered. *Cancer* – conquered. And the enemy that had gripped my heart for years, *death*, had been conquered most of all. It was hard to go through what I felt on the *Rock of Agony*, but Jesus' story didn't end there. The best was yet to come. And with my best friends passing away, I had dwelled far too long on my own rock of agony. But just as there was more to be told in the story of Jesus, my story doesn't have to end there either. The best is yet to come. Because just like that sign in the tomb of Jesus; Stephen and Kevin are *more alive* in Christ than ever before.

I stepped out of the tomb with a different perspective on life. I had been brought to Israel to see my *best friend's* home. But as much as God had transformed my life by *walking with me* all those years; there may have been an even greater change when I chose to *walk with Him.* From the tomb, we stepped outside to take communion together as a group. As I held out in front of me the bread and the wine, I couldn't help but feel the warmth of Jesus' smile. It wasn't a time of sadness or reflection of pain; it was a moment of *victorious* celebration in what He came to do for me ... and for *you.* And as I began to chew on the bread, I couldn't help but whisper soft expressions of gratitude under my breath, "Thank you for bringing me to your home, Jesus. Thank you for conquering death. Thank you that the best is truly yet to come." But just as I was about to drink from the cup, I raised it in front of me and said, *"But most of all, Jesus, thank you for being my best friend."*

Some have lost friends, some have lost brothers, and some have lost fathers. Everyone's journey is different. But there is one thing that remains the same. God longs to become what you've lost in your life. For me, it was a best friend, but for you, it could be different. But in every circumstance, there is a God who will stop at nothing to bring you hope. I felt like I was drowning in the depths of life; so God took me halfway around the planet to prove a point. While in Israel, I had the opportunity to swim in the Dead Sea, where I learned that the land elevation is the lowest in all the world; and its water is so salty that it makes you float to the surface. But as I stepped into the waters of that Dead Sea, I heard the phrase,

"Even at your lowest –
I will lift you up."

If I had to boil down the message of this book into nine simple words, those would be it: *"Even at your lowest, I will lift you up."* There's a popular phrase in society that refers to a dog as *Man's best friend,* but as you set this book down, I want you to look at the title in a similar way — except that I want you to read it out loud as if it were a common phrase heard in Heaven. *God's Best Friend.* And know that every single time that phrase is spoken, it's always in reference to *you.* There's an open invitation. – And those same words that called out to me are now being spoken over you. *"I will be your best friend."*

Prepare for the adventure of a lifetime. And enjoy the victory. God bless.

CPSIA information can be obtained
at www.ICGtesting.com
Printed in the USA
FSHW02n2057120918
52259FS